The *Greatest* Guide to Home-based

101 Great Business Ideas plus How to Work from Home

Written by Peter Hingston and Eric Smith

Front Cover Photographs   The photograph of the couple is Copyright © Tony Stone Images. The background photograph of a Potton home is Copyright © Richard Crisp of Potton Ltd.

Other Copyrights:

General: The chapters "Making it Legal" and "Coping with Taxation" and the "Tax Data Page" together with other material are taken and adapted from *The Greatest Little Business Book* by Peter Hingston.

Accounts Books   The sample accounts books pages shown on pages 47 and 50-52 are Copyright © 1991 by Peter Hingston and are reproduced with his permission.

Cartoons   The cartoons are Copyright © 1995 by Phil Anderton and are reproduced with his permission.

Note 1   In the worked examples in this book, all persons, companies and businesses are fictitious.

Note 2   Where a business or company is mentioned in this book, this does not imply any approval or recommendation of that business or company or their products or services.

Important   Although we have tried to ensure the accuracy of information in this book, no responsibility for loss occasioned to any person acting or refraining from action as a result of material in this book can be accepted by the authors or publisher. Due to the complexities involved when starting or running a business, we strongly advise the reader to take professional advice before making any decisions.

Comments   Although the authors welcome constructive comments or suggestions (some of which have been incorporated in this book), they are not able to handle queries relating to readers' personal business matters. These queries are best referred to a local business development unit, professional adviser or relevant government department.

Copyright © 1997 by Peter Hingston and Eric Smith. All rights reserved. 2nd Edition.
Reprinted: 1998 with minor updates.   First Edition: Copyright © 1995.

Based on the original book "Making Money At Home" published by Schwartz & Wilkinson in Australia and copyright © 1991 by Eric Smith. This adaptation, with extensive new material for the U.K. by Peter Hingston, published in the U.K. by Hingston Publishing Co. with kind permission of Schwartz & Wilkinson, Melbourne.

Published by Hingston Publishing Co.,
Honeymoor Lodge, Eaton Bishop, Hereford HR2 9QT.
Telephone: 01981 251621.

Printed in Great Britain by Hobbs the Printers Limited.

ISBN 0 906555 19 1

Introduction

When I was visiting Australia I came across Eric Smith's excellent book "Making Money At Home". His book was very easy to read and full of useful information, the only problem, from my viewpoint, being that it had been written solely for the Australian market.

I had for some time wanted to write a book on this very same subject so I made contact with Eric and his publishers who very kindly agreed for me to adapt his book for publication in Britain. The task proved a little more difficult than anticipated due to the differences in laws and market conditions so the final book has turned out to be very different from the original.

This book is in three distinct sections – the first discusses what it will be like starting a small business from home; the second section gets into essential business details such as the legalities and the third section features over a hundred interesting business ideas to inspire you.

While researching these business ideas we talked to many people around Britain who are running their own home-based businesses and they kindly shared their experiences with us.

Please don't feel you have to read this book from cover to cover, just dip into the part which is likely to be of immediate interest.

If you have not already made contact with your local Business Link (in England), Business Shop (in Scotland) or Enterprise Agency (located everywhere in the UK), remember they are there to help you and much of their advice is free.

I wish you every success with your venture.

P. Hingston

Acknowledgements

Authors' Acknowledgements

The collection of information necessary to produce a guide requires the co-operation of many individuals and organisations. To them our grateful thanks.

In particular, we would like to thank **Charlotte Hingston** and **Jimmy Walker** for their detailed proof reading and many constructive suggestions. We would also like to thank **Charlotte Hingston** for her help with the cover design. Thanks also to **Phil Anderton** who created the excellent cartoons, presented most professionally, for this book.

In addition, we would like to thank the following individuals who all contributed in some way or other. Those who run their own home-based businesses were generous in both the time and information they were prepared to give us. Listed in alphabetical order:
Anne Addison; Caroline Alexander; Kay Fielding; Elaine Fletcher; Bill Goodall; Irene Goodall; George and Anne Gow; Judy Greig; John Murray; Vicky O'Donnell; John Raith; Stuart Ramsden; John Robinson; Liz Woolfall.

Organisations who kindly provided useful information and who we would like to thank, include:
The British Franchise Association; The Crafts Council; Direct Selling Association; DSS (Contributions Agency), Perth; DTI Press Office (London); Environmental Health, Perth; Tayside Trading Standards Department.

Picture Credits

Photograph on page 63 with thanks to Neale Woolfall; photo on page 67 kindly provided by the Edinburgh Tourist Board; photo on page 68 from Peter Hingston's sports car photo archive; photo on page 72 kindly provided by The British School of Motoring Ltd; photo on page 76 with thanks to John Robinson; photo on page 77 kindly provided by Land Rover and photo on page 87 kindly provided by ADT Auctions.

Chapter: Business Ideas – Arts & Crafts We are grateful to the Crafts Council for its permission to quote some of the findings of its study "Crafts in the 1990s".

Contents

Why Start a Small Business?

IT sounds wonderful. Own your own business, make heaps of money, retire while you are young enough to enjoy it. Who could ask for more? Unfortunately it is not that simple. If all goes well, owning and managing your own business can be very rewarding. If things go wrong, it can be extremely difficult and it could even destroy you financially.

Whether your business succeeds or fails depends partly on things within your control, such as your judgement, initiative and capacity for work. However, things outside your control such as economic conditions, competition and government regulations can be just as important.

Your chances of success are better if you prepare yourself properly in the first place and consider the kind of problems that you are going to meet as the owner and manager of a business. The first thing that you need to get clear is why you are starting your own business at great risk to your pocket and sanity.

WHY START A BUSINESS?

There are many reasons why people go into business for themselves. Some of the reasons are good and some are bad. Five good reasons are:

1. To earn a better living If you have a talent to sell, it is much more satisfying and rewarding getting the full benefit of what you do. When you think about it, the only reason that someone employs you is that you can produce more income for them than you cost them in wages. With a little organisation on your part you can tap into the full value of your efforts.

2. To be independent It can be very frustrating working for someone else and not being allowed to make your own decisions. It has often been said that "it is worth thousands just to have the satisfaction and freedom of being your own boss".

3. To do something different Many surveys have found that relatively few people find satisfaction and enjoyment in their work. Doing something different, anything different, can be very appealing. Unfortunately, it can also blind people to the problems that they are likely to encounter.

4. To escape job frustration Frustration at work can arise out of lack of promotion, troubles with the boss, silly rules and coping with the people you have to deal with every day. Giving up a job because of this only makes sense if you can be sure that you will not strike similar situations in your own business.

5. To create your own job To a certain extent some people who go into business for themselves are buying themselves a job. They are setting up a business to provide them with employment because they are having difficulty in finding or holding a job.

There are also bad reasons for going into business for yourself. For example, there are people who go into business in order to avoid dealing with the general public. Often, people who work in shops become very frustrated with having to deal with customers and cope with a very demanding boss. When you go into your own business this will not end. You will find even greater demands placed on you by people every day.

Another poor reason for going into business is that you think it will be much easier than working for someone else. If this is the way you feel, forget it. It is almost certainly going to be much harder. The hours will be longer, the benefits that you will get as an owner, for some years at least, are certain to be less than those you would get as an employee. *"You will probably have to work very long hours and for a number of years you may well find that you make very little money out of the business at all".*

You have to take a long term view if you are going into business for yourself. There are very few business situations where you will make a lot of money very quickly. It is not unusual for small business people to work seven days a week and to work most weeks of the year, at least for the first five years of the business (Note: 5 years, not 5 months!). You will also find that it might be very difficult to take substantial amounts of money out of the business without severely damaging it. So, you may well

Creating your own job!

Why Start a Small Business?

find that not only do you have to work long hours but you also have to be satisfied with very small returns.

THE MAIN REQUIREMENTS OF BEING SELF-EMPLOYED

It is said that one requirement for running your own business is a good sense of humour because laughing is better than crying. There are other desirable characteristics too for a self-employed person – see right.

If you do not have *all* of these requirements, you need to think again about whether you really want to be in business for yourself. You must be honest about your own attitude to what you are doing.

Sometimes people go into business because their family or friends say something to them like, "You really should go into business for yourself because you make magnificent chairs"; or "Your paintings are beautiful, why don't you sell them through galleries and give up your job?"

What they do not realise is that there is a lot more to being in your own business than just being able to make or do something. Making magnificent chairs does not in itself create a business for you. What you have to be able to do is not just make your own chairs, *but make money out of making your own chairs*.

And certainly if you are not going to be getting an income from another job, you will have to make substantial money from it. This means that you must know how to market your product and be able to manage your finances.

Rules, Rules, Rules . . .

Being self-employed does not give you carte-blanche to do as you please and to ride rough-shod over your fellow

**PERSONALITY OF THE SUCCESSFUL BUSINESS PERSON
(Ask yourself: Have you got what it takes?)**

While it is difficult to generalise about what personality traits a successful business person must have, there are certain traits that are desirable in self-employed people, such as:

The desire to achieve   Most small business people are placed under tremendous stress from time to time and, if you do not have enough desire to achieve what you set out to do, it is very easy to give up. Some people give up right on the brink of a major breakthrough.

Motivation   You must be well motivated but if the members of your immediate family are not supportive of your idea of going into business for yourself, you will find it very difficult.

Self-Discipline   You must set yourself specific goals, and then work single-mindedly towards achieving them.

Technical competence   It is no good getting yourself involved in a business that you do not fully understand. Apart from anything else, if you do not have the competence and you are charging for what you do, you may be liable to be sued by dissatisfied customers. This could lose you far more money than you will ever earn from the business.

Good judgement   You need to be able to judge both business situations and people. In business you will have to deal with customers, suppliers, professional advisers and maybe employees. Experts say that decisiveness is another key factor to good management.

Intelligence   You must be reasonably intelligent. That does not mean that you have to be a genius. Geniuses by and large are not good business people. Probably, when we talk about intelligence here, we mean "street wise", the ability to exercise sufficient cunning and knowledge to keep ahead of the field.

Courage   There will be many occasions when you will need to draw heavily on your courage, particularly in the early stages of your business, when a lot of forces will be against you and good old guts and determination will be what keeps you going. There will also be occasions when a bold decision may mark a turning point in your business.

Initiative   You need to be able to take new initiatives, grasp opportunities and do things for yourself. If you have been employed by someone else you are probably used to being told what to do. When you are in your own business nobody will be telling you what to do. In fact, in many cases you will be expected to tell someone else what to do and to give direction.

Confidence   No-one can give you self-confidence. It can be built up only by being absolutely sure that you know what you are doing and by increasing experience. Giving an appearance of confidence, even if you don't always feel it, is extremely important.

Energy   You must be energetic in your approach to what you do. If you sit back and act in a passive way, letting things happen around you and making no effort to lead through your energy and effectiveness, then your business will suffer and any employees will also lack energy. However, do not confuse energy with aggression.

Honesty   Honesty is often under-rated. Business is not about ripping people off. In fact, in most cases unless you are honest you will not last long in business.

Emotional stability   Don't lose your temper. To do so with employees can be very harmful and losing your temper with customers will probably lose you business. And try not to worry about your business to the point where it makes you ill.

Cautiousness   Look before you leap and ensure you have an escape route.

Why Start a Small Business?

citizens in your drive for success.

However, there are a few people who try to get away with whatever they can, ignoring regulations which they feel are simply there for other people.

Thankfully, most people in business are reasonably honest. In the short run, there are times when those who play entirely by the rules may find it difficult to compete. However, in the long run, only ethical, honest business people prosper.

A word of warning – don't play any games with the Inland Revenue or H.M. Customs & Excise (VAT) because they play the game very hard. Remember that every time you stray from the rules you are taking another risk and if you get caught you probably will not think it was worth it.

THE RISKS YOU WILL TAKE

In setting up a business it is very difficult to avoid risk. Most people do not like taking risks but when you go into business you face four main risks:

1. Financial Strain

There is a real risk of financial difficulties and possibly even financial failure. When starting your own business, you will probably invest a substantial part of your life savings and you may be required to mortgage your home or offer it as security for the finance used in the business. At the very least you and your family may have to accept a lower standard of living until the business becomes established.

These risks are worthwhile if the business eventually becomes profitable and you can remove any liabilities which were placed upon the home. However, if the business fails, many people will actually lose most of what they originally owned.

IT'S EASY TO UNDERESTIMATE HOW MUCH BUSINESS KNOW-HOW IS NECESSARY JUST TO SURVIVE IN BUSINESS

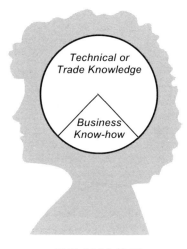

COMMON MYTH

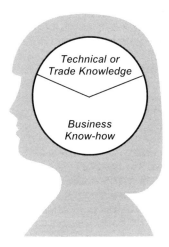

TYPICAL REALITY

2. Career Interruption

You may have been in a job for a number of years and be quite well established in that firm. Such security of employment is something of value to you but you will be risking that when you start your own business. Certainly if your business fails you will have a lot of difficulty getting another job at the same level as the one you gave up. Most likely you will have to start at a lower level. So there is a risk that, by interrupting your career, you may not achieve as high a level of seniority as you would have otherwise.

3. Family Problems

There is a risk of straining family relationships. It can be very stressful starting and operating a small business. It makes tremendous demands on your energy, your emotions and your time. Time, energy and feelings devoted to the business cannot also be devoted to your family. From time to time members of the family may feel that they are being ignored or even neglected and you will probably have to make a substantial effort to ensure that they do not feel this too strongly.

4. Personal Failure

If you fail in business this may destroy your own confidence. You may have gone through life up to that time succeeding in most things that you have done. The impact on your own personality of a major failure in business may be very severe. It may make you feel inadequate. When this happens to some people they find it difficult to start working effectively

Why Start a Small Business?

again or to retain a normal personal life.

These are just some of the risks that are involved. If you are going into business you should fully discuss these risks with your family and any other people who will be affected by your decisions. Of course, although the risks are great the rewards can also be great. There are many things that you can get from being in business for yourself which are difficult to achieve if you spend your whole life as an employee of someone else.

THE BENEFITS YOU MAY REAP

Personal Satisfaction   There is a great deal of satisfaction to be gained in facing risks and succeeding against tremendous odds. If you are one of the comparatively rare breed of people who does well in business, it will give your ego a wonderful boost.

Financial Rewards   It has often been said that there are few millionaire employees. If you want to reach the financial heights then you have to take risks and you do not take those risks as an employee. The financial rewards can be very great but this is only because the risk level is so high.

Sense of achievement   There is a usually a great sense of achievement in succeeding in what you do and a pride in being able to look at it and say "I did that". However, a word of warning. Some people like to knock those who are successful. Also, your immediate family may still give you less recognition for what you achieve than will others. So do not expect them to look upon you with awe and admiration.

Social Recognition   There is an element in society which regards people who succeed in their own businesses as leaders in the community. And there is another element that regards such people as having exploited workers in some way. However, the social recognition that arises out of conducting your own successful business is usually something to be enjoyed. It can, for example, lead to a career as a councillor in local politics, if that appeals to you.

Sense of Freedom   One of the worst things about working for others is that you are usually given lots of instructions about what you are allowed to do and what you are not allowed to do. This can often be very frustrating. In your own business you will have the freedom to make your own decisions. But for some people this means the freedom to make their own mistakes. When you make the decisions, you have to live with the results.

Chance to create Jobs   We have already said that many people who start their own businesses are virtually buying a job. They are creating a job for themselves because they have had difficulty getting one or fear that they may become unemployed again in the future. Starting your own business can also create employment for other members of your family and the local community, which can be very satisfying.

A FULL TIME JOB or JUST SOME EXTRA CASH?

You need to have your business intentions clear in your mind. Do you want a business that can fully support you or is it simply to provide some additional income? This book covers both options.

Do you intend the business to start in a small way from home but hope to grow it into a larger business operating one day from "conventional" business premises? Or are you content with leaving it as a home-based business?

When you talk to people in business about how they came to be doing what they are now, it is amazing how often they started out on one path and along the way their business completely altered course ∎

The Good News and Bad News

IN a perfect world you wouldn't have to work at all. But the next best thing must be working from home, mustn't it? After all, there will be no problems about travelling to and from work in busy traffic, and no boss standing over you making you do things that you do not particularly want to do. There must be a wonderful sense of freedom in being able to spend your time in the way that you want. However, this is the up-side of the situation.

The Down-Side Being your own boss can be very demanding. You have to be prepared to work for realistic goals; you must have self discipline, persistence and determination to succeed. Working from home can create additional strains and obligations and create problems for your family.

Isolation For a start you have the problem of social isolation. You are not going to be meeting as many people every day in your job as you would if you were employed by someone else. It can lead to boredom and loneliness particularly if you are accustomed to a lively environment. You will also miss the stimulation of working with colleagues. *Note:* This drawback can be a lot more significant than it seems at first glance.

Work/Family Life Clash There is also the problem of combining work and family life in the one place. Some members of your family are likely to be more demanding of your time simply because you are at home. They may have some difficulty in understanding that just because you are at home it does not mean that you are not working. It is very difficult to combine running a home with running a business unless you are realistic about the things you hope to achieve. The distractions

"That's the worst thing about working from home – the traffic jams in the morning!"

can cause severe disruption to your business and can lead to frustrations which can easily destroy your business activity. It is very easy in a home business situation to take the attitude that what is not done today can easily be put off until tomorrow and this can again mean that your business does not grow in the way it should.

HOME-BASED BUSINESSES

Despite the problems that we have mentioned and a lot more that we have yet to mention, there is a large range of businesses that can be operated from home. Some of the possibilities are:

Services Businesses that provide a service, rather than making things, are the largest group of home-based businesses. This is because there are many regulations and practical difficulties in

manufacturing and trading from home which do not apply to services.

These services range from running a cleaning business through to the most sophisticated computer programming and medical services. Some of the typical service businesses that are conducted from home include:

● *Professions* such as accountants, doctors, dentists, veterinary surgeons, architects, all types of consultants and financial advisers.

● *Trades* like plumbers, electricians, painters & decorators and washing machine repairs.

● *Information-based services* like free-lance writers, typing, secretarial and people who provide computer services.

● *Domestic and household services* such as gardening, lawnmowing, house

The Good News and Bad News

maintenance, cleaning and handyman jobs and babysitting.

● *Personal or educational services* such as giving music lessons or providing tuition for students who are trying to get through examinations at all levels. Coaching of all kinds, including sports and relaxation skills, are also possible.

Retailing There are some small mail-order businesses which are operated from home. Personal network selling, eg by party-plan, is another possible home-based activity. What you cannot do is open a shop in your home, unless you get planning permission, which is unlikely in a residential area.

Manufacturing Quite obviously heavy manufacturing or large-scale manufacturing is out of the question in a residential area. Within the constraints of the legalities mentioned in the later chapter **Making it Legal**, you may be able to make craft products of various kinds, produce wooden toys, do printing or dressmaking. Perhaps in some

---

Some Advantages Of Being A Small Home-Based Business

The Customer May Get:

1. Fast, personal service
2. Personal guarantee of quality
3. Direct access to "boss" (i.e. you)
4. Friendly discussion
5. Flexibility
6. Ease of dealing with any complaints
7. Better prices due to lower overheads
8. Possible access to you out-of-hours
9. Convenience (if you are local)

---

limited circumstances it may be possible to do sub-assembly work for other factories or making up for people in the garment industry.

IS YOUR BUSINESS IDEA SUITABLE FOR YOUR HOME?

Not every type of business can be home-based. There are a number of questions which you need to consider, such as:

"Is the business going to be noisy?"
"Will the business create a smell?"
"Is there anything else about the proposed business that is likely to disrupt or upset the neighbours?"

If the answer to any of these questions is *"Yes"*, it is highly unlikely that you will be able to conduct that business from home for any length of time. For example, one individual started making wooden toys in his garage in the evening after work. The garage was fairly soundproof and he thought that there would be no effect on his neighbours. However, his electric saw and other machinery caused interference with the TV reception of his neighbours. He did not even know it was happening until they complained. Needless to say, this put a stop to his work.

It may well be that the storage of material for the business is unsightly and neighbours complain that their enjoyment of the residential area is being disrupted by the presence of this material. Or, they may claim that it harbours rats or other vermin.

You must realise that there are many people in this world who seem dedicated to stopping anything new. This kind of person finds it difficult to understand your strange thinking, that you want to be productive, to create things. Rarely will you beat them if you come

into direct conflict so the best approach may be to make sure that you do not draw attention to yourself.

Location

If your business requires that clients visit your home this creates further problems. First, you need to consider your location. Is your home difficult to get to or to find or in an area which is not very accessible? If it is, then of course you would not want to conduct the type of home business that requires frequent visits from clients. As an example, if you were thinking about running a secretarial venture from home and you live in an area where there is limited parking and clients need to visit you, then quite clearly that is a problem.

Even if you do have parking nearby, will there be so many visitors that it could create parking problems in the street? Certainly, if that is the case, neighbours will soon complain. In such a case it is likely that you will be stopped from conducting your business activity from home. There is no good reason why your neighbours should suffer just because you are conducting your business in a residential area.

Credibility

Although customers may accept that certain types of business can be home-based, they may be less happy dealing with other businesses if they knew they were being operated from someone's house. Lack of credibility can therefore be a real problem, especially if your potential customers are government organisations or large corporations.

Keeping in Touch

You should also consider whether the type of work that you have in mind requires frequent contact with other people in your field in order to keep you up to date. If this is the case then running a business from home may not be a good idea. If your business is at the cutting edge of new technology, you may slip behind by being away from others working in the same area. However, this may be overcome through reading technical journals, visiting trade shows and by joining business organisations in your field.

IS YOUR HOME SUITABLE FOR A BUSINESS?

Even if your business idea is suitable for being home-based, your own home may not be suitable. Some of the questions that need to be answered are:

1. Is there adequate working space in your home? At the very least you need a table and pencil holder in the corner of a spare room.

If possible, try to avoid setting aside a room (or garage) that is to be used exclusively for your business. Although this may be a very practical solution, be aware that it could have important tax implications as it may make that room (or garage) liable to Business Rates and there could be Capital Gains Tax implications if and when you sell your home – get expert advice from an accountant.

2. Are there legal constraints? Houses are generally regarded as homes, not places of work. Refer to "Property Problems" in the chapter **Making it Legal** and get advice from a solicitor on this important aspect.

3. Is there a separate entrance for clients? If your clients need to visit you, then ideally you do not want them coming to the same door as your friends and perhaps the friends of your children. Each group will get in the other's way and you will have an equal number of complaints from members of your family and potential clients. So it is better if these two groups can be kept separate from each other.

4. Does your house have adequate parking? It will offend your neighbours very quickly if you do not provide your own parking unless there is plenty of local parking. There is nothing worse than arriving home to find someone is parked across your driveway; or never being able to park outside your own home because there are always people there who are visiting someone else. You can be sure that your neighbours will know what you are doing. Giving them a valid reason to report your activities or make a complaint is to be avoided. If you have employees you should ensure there is adequate parking for them also.

5. Do you have a separate business phone line? It is not too expensive to get a separate phone line installed for the business. You don't really want your personal and business calls coming in on the same phone, particularly if you have teenage children.

6. Does your home have adequate storage space? If the business requires significant amounts of stock to be stored then quite obviously this might be a problem in many homes and is worth thinking about at this early stage.

7. Do you have a wide enough letter-box? If you are expecting a lot of business mail it certainly helps if you have a letter-box that is wide enough to cope with large envelopes.

If you have not provided for these practical things, then you need to do so before you start your business. It is no good fooling yourself that it will not be a problem and that you will be able to sort out the situation as you go along. It will not happen that way.

However, before you even consider costly home alterations, it would be a very good idea to consult a lawyer to ensure that the changes you are planning are legal and an accountant to ensure that the tax position (in terms of both liabilities and possible allowable expenses) is clearly established.

INVOLVING YOUR FAMILY IN THE BUSINESS

One of the joys of operating a business from home is that the whole family can become involved. In some instances this works particularly well. However, there are situations where family members can be a hindrance rather than a help in the operation of the business. You need to give a lot of thought to

The Good News and Bad News

the way in which the business will impact on your family and the way in which your family will impact on the business. Let us consider some of the matters which might arise . . . .

Children and the Business Some people claim that children can be a real asset to the business, for instance they can answer the phone and help with packaging and other simple tasks. But others feel they are best kept away from customers who would probably prefer to deal with adults. The presence of children may make some customers feel the business is unprofessional.

It works the other way too. Children often resent the operation of a business from their home, particularly where potential clients are arriving regularly. No sooner do your children have your attention than you have to deal with some client and you have not got time for them. As a good general rule children and business do not mix, so if you think it is going to be an ideal existence playing with your children and operating a business at the same time, forget it. Unless you are very fortunate there is little chance that you will be able to do those two things together.

Other Members of the Family In some business situations it is possible for the husband and wife, or partners, to work as a team. This is very common in service industries where one person provides the service and the other operates the office from home, acting as secretary, book-keeper and receptionist. This is fine so long as you do not have a situation where one person (often the man) is out all day and the partner (usually the woman) is entirely stuck in the home.

To avoid this problem it may be best to have a telephone answering machine so that the person who is at home is able to get away for at least part of the day.

Watching for Strains There is no doubt that owning a business puts extra strains on family relationships and the pressure of business can certainly put a strain on any marriage. There is a double strain if the business is being operated from the home because you have the other problems that we have already mentioned.

Running a business from home may solve the problem of the person whose previous job meant they were away from home for long periods. However, just because the person running the business is at home does not necessarily make them accessible to other members of the family. It may well be in some cases that if the business was instead operated from an office there would be just as much time available for the family.

RELATIONSHIPS WITH YOUR NEIGHBOURS

Some people who operate home businesses have a bad reputation with their neighbours. This often arises through lack of thought and failure to see the situation from the neighbour's point of view. There are four major aspects of the home business which might cause problems with neighbours (and hence the authorities): (1) Visitors and the associated problem of car parking; (2) Noise; (3) Air pollution eg fumes and (4) Visual pollution, i.e. having a mess outside your house.

Despite all of these potential problems many hundreds of thousands of people conduct successful, happy businesses from their homes. So we are not suggesting that you forget the whole idea simply because of the potential

---

SPACE – THE FINAL FRONTIER (of your home)

To run a business from your home you need S P A C E:

Space to Work In This could be simply the corner of a room, or the occasional use of the kitchen table. A filing cabinet is useful to keep all your business records in one place.

Space to Meet Clients If you need to meet clients then you will have to consider where that is possible. Some home-based businesses get around this problem by meeting at the client's premises or if that is not possible, they use hotel facilities.

Space for Storage This has already been mentioned, but can represent a significant problem. In most cities you can rent storage space by the month.

---

problems. We are simply suggesting that planning in advance and being realistic about the way in which things are going to proceed is much better than fooling yourself that there will be no problems.

Often the key is consultation and discussion with everyone who is likely to be affected. This will prevent misunderstandings and difficulties which may otherwise prove very serious ∎

Getting Started in Your Business

EVERY successful business was once just an idea in someone's mind. Converting an idea into a profitable business is not easy. However it should be a lot easier if you follow this simple ten-point formula:

1. Find something which your community needs then provide it. Whether it is a service or a product, the need must be there, waiting to be filled. In a small business you cannot afford the expensive advertising necessary to create a market in the way that is done with a mass selling product.

2. Check the legal implications of what you intend to do. Is it legal? Is a licence required? Refer to the following chapter **Making it Legal** and get professional advice.

3. Carry out some simple market research. This doesn't mean you have to go to a specialist market research organisation and pay large amounts of money finding out about your particular activity. Find out for yourself who your customers are likely to be. Find out where they live and what they do; who they are and what their spending power is. Try to understand your market as well as you can. Even big companies can sometimes make mistakes in their market research. There is a classic story about an American manufacturer of cake mixes who decided they would target the Japanese market. To the cake mix, all you had to do was add an egg, some milk and put it in the oven. Twenty minutes later you would have a fresh cake on the table. They even went to the trouble of developing special recipes for Japan. However, a little more research would have told them that Japanese houses seldom have ovens. Their target market just could not use the cake mixes!

That error cost the company millions of dollars. You are not involved with millions but neither do you have money to waste in making false assumptions about your potential market.

4. Assess the competition. Is anybody already doing what you are thinking of doing? If they are, why would people transfer to your business? Look at both direct and indirect competition.

Direct competition is with someone who is already providing those goods or services. Indirect competition is where your goods or services are not identical but you are still competing with them indirectly. For example, a wallpapering service competes indirectly with painters and businesses that supply wood veneer sheets. Your competition is always much broader than you first realise.

5. Make a realistic assessment of your likely sales figures. How much do you realistically believe you could earn in the first month, quarter, half year and year? Be honest with yourself in these estimates because the only person you are fooling is yourself. If you set unrealistically high sales figures then you may fool yourself into putting your savings and future into something which in reality is a flop. People often do this, even though their subconscious may be screaming at them not to do it, because they do not want to let go of a dream. So, perhaps it is best to be a little more pessimistic than you really think is warranted when estimating the figures.

6. Estimate the major costs. Again do not be over-optimistic. You are only cheating yourself if you estimate your expenses at lower levels than you really know they will be.

KEY POINT A major cause of business failure is under-funding, i.e. people start a business with less capital than they really need. As a result, the money runs out and the business folds.

The chapter **Preparing a Mini Business Plan** contains a "fill-in-the-blanks" form to list your start-up costs. When completing this form, remember that Murphy's Law will prevail . . . *"If something can go wrong, it will, and what is more it will go wrong at the worst possible moment"*.

Getting Started in Your Business

When you have got the final figure, add a contingency. This is an allowance for the hundreds of things that you have not thought of and for costs being higher than budgeted (which is usually the case).

7. Prepare a business plan. A later chapter explains how to do this. It is extremely important. It is as relevant for the smallest micro business as it is for a large corporation. Only by preparing a business plan can you give yourself an accurate guide as to where you are going and what you expect to do. It should give you a realistic estimate of the returns that are going to come from the business. It is also a valuable indication to bankers and others that you know what you are doing.

8. Collect a set of good advisers. Gather around you a set of advisers and helpers who will genuinely be of assistance to you. (We cover this in more detail – see opposite).

9. Advertise and seek free promotion. Do not spend heavily on this. Going into a small business and using expensive TV advertising with the hope that it will lead to a big increase in your sales is unlikely to work. Long before your sales catch up with your expenditure you will be out of business. You are not in the business of selling to everyone in the whole country, you are more likely to be in the business of selling to a particular group which may even be localised in your area.

You should keep your promotional costs as low as possible. If you understand your target market you will know the best place to promote and the most effective way to spend your money.

Free promotion may be available by telling local newspapers about the service you provide or the unusual goods you have for sale. A small advertisement may lead to a feature article in the same local newspaper. This article which costs you nothing is much more valuable than the advertisement.

10. Expect to start slowly. Develop your activities steadily and do not try to take too much money out of the business. Plough the money back in to generate more activity. If you really want your business to grow then you can probably forget about getting any real income out of it for at least the first year or more. In some cases it may be three to five years before you can afford to take out profits.

KEY POINT

If you need to take a lot of cash from your business to meet domestic bills, this will put a severe strain on your business.

THE BUSINESS IDEA?

All businesses hatch out of an initial idea.

Finding the right niche in the market to fill is a critical decision on the way to making your nest egg. First of all, start by thinking about your own needs.

What would you like someone else to do for you that you have to do for yourself at the moment? Have you ever been in a situation where you desperately needed a product and could not get it? Or, are there situations where you can get the product but the service is very poor; or do you have to wait longer than you believe is reasonable? Is the quality not good enough? Is the price too high?

Think long and deeply about this so that you put together a range of possibilities without becoming too committed to one particular course of action.

Having done that you could read through the business ideas section which forms a major part of this book. Mark those businesses that you think you could do even if you don't believe at this stage that it is something you would choose to do. Perhaps this will jog your memory about some of the things that you could have considered, some of the services that you wished were more available to you. From this information prepare a list of possibilities.

On a separate sheet write down your own skills, abilities and interests. What are the things that you like to do? And what are the things that you could spend all of your time doing? Or even part of your time doing? If your business is going to develop you are going to spend a lot of time doing the thing that represents the source of your income, so it is best to enjoy it.

Then talk to people. Talk to people in business, your neighbours and relatives. Talk to local business people and find out how their businesses are going. Find out what services they wish they had which are not available to them. Draw on as many sources of information as you possibly can. However, *a word of caution:* it is probably best to float your idea with people in general terms rather than letting them know in detail what you are going to do.

Members of your own family may be, unexpectedly, very negative about your ideas and they may discourage you. It may be an excellent idea but you may be put off by the attitude of friends and family. However, listen to what they say by way of genuine arguments both for and against the idea. There are many examples of people who have been talked out of excellent ideas only to see someone else take them and do well. On the other hand, you should not cling to your precious idea against over-whelming evidence that perhaps, maybe perhaps, it is not such a good idea after all.

Often, people become heavily committed to a course of action too early in the game. This can lead to failure because they have been so committed to the idea that, when they worked out their business plan, they actually fudged the figures to make it look like an attractive proposition simply to convince themselves and others that they should go ahead with it. Try hard to avoid this situation.

If you know someone who is already doing something similar to what you have in mind, speak to them about how well it is going. Of course, you should not expect completely honest answers. If they are doing particularly well with their business and you come along and say "Look, I'm thinking of starting the same kind of business as you. How is it going?" They would not want you to compete with them. So, you are not likely to get a straight answer. If their business is going well they are likely to talk it down to discourage you and if it is going badly they may well exaggerate its success to save face or in the hope of selling their business to you. So you

must be cautious in these circumstances and be a reasonable judge of human nature.

PROFESSIONAL HELP

If you are only in business to make a little pocket money then you will probably manage without much expert advice. But if you expect your business to be full-time then it's very important to develop an early working relationship with a good accountant, banker, business adviser, insurance broker and a solicitor (listed here in alphabetical order):

Accountants   You will almost certainly need an accountant to give you advice when you start your business. They can help you with taxation matters, your pricing, how you are going to keep your accounts (i.e. the book-keeping) and can give general business advice. In addition they can act on your behalf in dealing with the Inland Revenue and can submit your annual Tax Return.

A good accountant is a very worthwhile asset but accountants do vary greatly in their abilities and in the time they are prepared to spend with each client – so choose one carefully!

An initial meeting with an accountant is usually free. Discuss with them your business plans and how you propose to keep your accounts (see also the chapter **Simple Book-Keeping** later in this book). In most cases a simple accounts book will probably be sufficient at first. Whatever system you use, you must always keep a record of all the *expenses* and all the *income* that comes from the business.

At your initial meeting with the accountant, ask for an indication of their likely annual fees. *Note:* If you are a sole

trader or partnership, there is no legal requirement to have an accountant do your Tax Return. In fact if your "turn-over" (i.e. your total annual sales) is less than a certain amount, then the Inland Revenue will accept what are called Simple Tax Accounts. This is explained in more detail on the **Tax Data Page** at the very end of this book.

However, unless your tax affairs are very simple and your business is just making a little pocket money, then the advice of an accountant is usually worthwhile to avoid errors or paying out unnecessary tax.

If you have been an employee in the past you may be blissfully unaware of how much tax you have been paying as you will have been paid the net amount by your employer. As a self-employed person you are in for a very rude awakening when you discover just how much tax you are paying! Tax rates of 20%, 25%, 40% or whatever may seem academic until you realise that of the big contract you have just won, worth let's say £2,000 in profit, you could be handing over £500 or even £800 to the Inland Revenue!

Bankers   Although you may or may not choose to discuss your business idea with your bank manager, they will almost certainly wish to see you when you ask to open a business account. In any event, there will be times when you will need some support from your bank. That is, access to the occasional loan or unsecured overdraft or perhaps some worthwhile financial advice.

You should keep your bank manager abreast of all major developments and plans you have for your business. They are careful people so do not frighten them with sudden changes of course and do not give them ultimatums such

Getting Started in Your Business

as "If I don't get the £5,000 overdraft tomorrow, I shall have to cease trading!" You should be planning sufficiently ahead to give them advance warning of such events.

You should visit your bank manager or at least phone or write to them every few months just to keep in touch. Many bankers have more business knowledge than you might expect, but as with any service, if you are unhappy with your bank, then consider changing branch or move to another bank. But do remember that it is usually worth staying with the bank that knows you.

Business Advisers These days there are a whole range of small business advisers who are ready and willing to help you. In fact the sheer number of organisations might be a little confusing particularly as their activities tend to overlap. The main organisations are (in alphabetical order):

British Steel (Industry) Ltd This organisation helps businesses to start up, expand or relocate in the traditional steel areas around the country. They provide loans and/or share capital in amounts from £10,000 to £150,000. They can also provide work space for small businesses in some of the areas. Tel: 0114 2731612.

Business Links It can be very confusing to know which business support agency to approach. In England, to solve this problem, over 200 Business Links have been created. They will answer your queries or put you in touch with the right people. The Business Links are a partnership of TECs, Chambers of Commerce, local authorities, local enterprise agencies and others. All the Department of Trade and Industry regional services are now provided through these Business Links. In Wales, there are **Business Connect** offices.

Business Shops These are "first-stop" shops located around Scotland (but excluding the Highlands and Islands, which has broadly similar **Business Information Source** offices). Guidance and information is available on subjects such as start-up, training, exporting, legal matters, finance, marketing and franchising etc.

Enterprise Agencies *(called Enterprise Trusts in Scotland)* These non-profit making organisations are often funded jointly by the local Private and Public Sectors and their aim is to encourage new and existing small businesses, providing mainly free business advice and much else besides. They work closely with the Business Links (or, in Scotland, the Business Shops). To find your nearest, look in the Yellow Pages.

Industrial Development Units Many local authorities have such units. They can provide business advice and usually have factory premises to rent. They can also advise on local planning and licencing matters.

LiveWIRE (now known as Shell Live-WIRE) If you are aged 16 to 30 and want to start your own business then Shell LiveWIRE can help with advice and if recently started you could also win £10,000 in their "Young Business Start Up" awards competition.

ADDRESS

Please refer to page 114 for addresses.

Getting Started in Your Business

Local Enterprise Companies (LECs)
These are business-led organisations in Scotland, formed to encourage enterprise, provide training and assist small firms, in addition to other related activities. Get the address of your own LEC from Scottish Enterprise.

Prince's Youth Business Trust This scheme was the Prince of Wales' own idea and he is its President. The Trust helps 18 to 30 year olds who are unemployed, under-employed or of limited means, to set up and run their own businesses.

The Prince's Youth Business Trust provides financial help (mainly by soft loans) for applicants who have a viable business idea, but who have been unsuccessful in raising the finance elsewhere to start their own venture.

An important feature is that each new business has their own "business mentor" appointed to help them and this help is ongoing.

The scheme is national with regional offices.

In Scotland, there is the Prince's Scottish Youth Business Trust (PSYBT) which has slightly different rules.

 Their addresses are given at the end of this book.

ADDRESS

Training & Enterprise Councils (TECs)
These are similar to the LECs (see above), but are found in England and Wales. Get the address of your own TEC from Yellow Pages.

Insurance Brokers Insurance is designed to protect you financially against losses by theft, damage, fire or other specified causes. It is also a legal requirement to have certain types of insurance, eg vehicle insurance and Employer's Liability Insurance (the latter only if you employ someone). You should therefore discuss your proposed venture with an insurance broker (who should be a registered insurance broker). You may only get an estimate of your likely insurance premiums at this early stage as you probably will not have the full details they require. The whole subject of insurance is covered in more detail in the next chapter in this book: **Making it Legal**.

Solicitors If you are going to run a small, simple, straightforward business you are unlikely to need much legal advice. However, it may still make good sense to see a solicitor when you set up your business and whenever you have legal queries. Thinking ahead and getting good advice early can prevent problems from getting bigger later on.

Identifying a good solicitor is difficult; as with accountants, a good one is a worthwhile asset. When you speak to the solicitor you are considering, ask questions. Ask what their commercial experience is and what the fees are likely to be. Certainly do not let high-ish fees scare you off. In the law profession, as in many other areas, you usually get what you pay for. Cheap advice could be very costly in the long run.

Remember that you should not waste any time when you are talking to a solicitor as you will be charged on a time basis. This usually applies as much to phone calls as it does to meetings. It is like having a meter ticking over while you are chatting. So prepare in advance, as far as possible, for any meeting or phone conversation.

You should certainly consider seeing a solicitor if you plan to take on a franchise or if you are asked to sign a contract with anyone, eg a Network Marketing company.

FOR "HOME", READ "WORKPLACE"

For most people starting their first business, their previous experience as an employee will mean that for them their home is a place where they can relax and dress casually. When they start working at home, there is scope for some mental confusion but this can easily be eliminated by *treating your home as your place of work during normal working hours*. So when you start your business, behave just as if you were leaving home each morning to go to a "normal" job.

"Hi Honey, I'm home!"

Getting Started in Your Business

To help you get in the right frame of mind for work, you should dress smartly in conventional business attire – not jeans and trainers! For non-office work the appropriate overalls, or whatever, should be worn.

At first glance this might seem a bit silly but it does really work. It has the additional benefit that if a business contact appears on your doorstep without any warning then you will not be caught out looking sloppy.

Another way to strengthen this "at work" feeling is to stick to rigid hours, eg 9am to 6pm, with a set break for lunch. This also helps other family members understand when you are supposed to be *working*.

You can reinforce this point by saying to the others each morning that you are "going to the office" or "starting work". And if they should suggest that you might like to stop and walk the dog or go shopping, remind them politely but firmly that you are *working!*

Some relatives, particularly older ones, will never fully understand the situation. Whereas they would never think of "just dropping in to see you" if you worked in an office or factory, they will happily arrive on your doorstep and expect a welcome, a coffee and a time-consuming chat. Some home-based business people may view this as one of the *benefits* of being self-employed and working at home. But such interruptions can also be very frustrating if you are trying to get on with some work.

What you will find is that after several years you can become more relaxed and less rigid about your dress, working hours and visitors ∎

BUSINESS BASICS

Chapters

ONCE you have completed your market research, the next step is to prepare a Business Plan, but before you can do that it is necessary to digress briefly to look at the essential legalities to consider when starting a business. Note that the law makes little distinction between running a micro business from the kitchen table which earns pocket money, and a giant corporation. So the rules and regulations, as they exist, usually apply to your small business as much as they do to any other business. It is important to speak to a solicitor at an early stage.

 CAUTION Please note this chapter is for general guidance only and should not be regarded as a complete or authoritative statement of the law. For more information, please consult a solicitor or the relevant authorities.

SOLE TRADER, PARTNERSHIP or LIMITED COMPANY?

An early decision is what legal form the business should take. If you are going to be a one-boss business you could be a "sole trader" (i.e. self-employed) or a "limited company" while if you and your spouse or partner are going into business together then you need to be a "partnership" or a "limited company". Some people think that they must form a limited company whenever they start in business but this is in fact rarely the case.

Sole Trader This is probably the most common legal form when a business starts. You can trade under your own name or a business name (see next page). You can also employ staff. Should the business fail owing money, then your creditors can seize your personal possessions to recover their losses. Many businesses start as "sole trader" but as they grow they change to a "limited company" status for two reasons: a) the limited liability protection given to their personal possessions and b) it is easier for them to raise larger sums of money for expansion.

Partnership If two or more people work together and no one is an "employee" then the law regards the arrangement as a "partnership", which has important consequences. Most importantly, each partner will be "jointly and severally liable" for any debts the business runs up. What this means in practice is if Partner A buys a car using a business cheque which subsequently bounces, the car dealer can pursue Partner B for the entire amount! Also, unless there is an agreement to the contrary, profits in a partnership have to be shared equally between partners.

It is a sad truth that many partners come to blows but this could be avoided if the partners started off with a good written Partnership Agreement.

 FURTHER READING A worked example of a Partnership Agreement is given in ***The Greatest Little Business Book.***

Choose your partner(s) carefully. They could lead to your personal bankruptcy just as easily as helping you to make a fortune. It may be better for them to be employees rather than partners.

In any partnership, consider taking out "cross insurance". This is a life assurance policy payable to the other partner(s) in the event of one partner dying to enable the surviving partner(s) to purchase the deceased partner's share of the business from his or her estate and to continue trading.

Limited Company Unlike a sole trader a limited liability company is a legal entity in its own right. Its shareholders and Directors may change but the company will continue to exist until wound up. Companies have many laws to regulate them and no one should consider setting up a company without fully understanding the implications and having taken professional advice.

A limited company used to require a minimum of two shareholders (who could be husband and wife) but now Single Member Companies are permitted.

A company must have at least one Director. The company must also have a company secretary (who could be a second Director, another shareholder, your accountant or your solicitor).

Limited Company or Sole Trader/Partnership?

Advantages of Ltd Co: Limited liability of Directors and shareholders, i.e. should the company fail, in most cases all you would lose is your share capital (unless you have signed personal guarantees or are guilty of some misdemeanour); easier to raise larger sums of money; easier format to cope with investors who do not want to work in the business; greater credibility with some customers.

Disadvantages of Ltd Co: Directors' wages subject to PAYE; overall taxation sometimes greater due to high National Insurance contributions; public disclosure of some key data; cannot offset losses against your previous income tax; cannot easily move funds in and out of your business bank account; onerous legal responsibilities on all Directors.

Making it Legal

Companies House (addresses listed on the right) produce a series of free small booklets which give more advice and are highly recommended reading.

Directors derive benefits by being paid a salary or fees while shareholders get paid "dividends" out of any profits.

You can buy an "off-the-shelf" company for around £150-£200 and this can be done within days. Only buy from a reputable company to ensure what you are buying is indeed a "clean" company without liabilities. Contact your solicitor or look under "Company Registration Agents" in the Yellow Pages.

Winding up a company, in contrast, can be a much more expensive and protracted process.

BUSINESS NAMES

A sole trader can trade under his own name (married name if a woman) i.e. as William Smith, W. Smith, Wm. Smith, Smith or William David Smith and a partnership can trade under the names of all the partners. But if a business name is to be used (eg "Smith's Giftshop") then the requirements of the Business Names Act 1985 apply. The Act prevents you from using certain words in a business name and regulates the disclosure of business ownership (as detailed below).

Sensitive Words   You cannot use any name for your business – it must not be offensive and the use of certain words needs approval, eg Limited (unless you are incorporated), International, National, British, Scottish, Irish, English, Welsh, European, Royal, Group, Trust, Society, Breeder, Registered etc. A list of such words and how you might get permission to use them is given in the booklets "Business Names and Business Ownership" and "Sensitive Words and Expressions" available from any Companies House.

Note that as there is no registration of business names, someone else might unintentionally use the same name unless you formed a limited company (as no two companies can have exactly the same name).

Disclosure of Ownership The Business Names Act also requires:

1. Business Stationery   All letterheads, orders, invoices, receipts, statements and demands must carry, in addition to the business name, the names of all the owners and in relation to each person named an address "at which documents can be served" (this is normally the business address). Refer also to the letterheads illustrated on page 27.

2. Business Premises Sign   This same information must be displayed prominently and legibly on a sign in all the places where you carry on your business and deal with customers or suppliers. There are no set rules as to the design of this sign but one suggestion is illustrated on the opposite page. Note that the size of the sign should be commensurate with its surroundings.

3. On Request   The names and the addresses of all owners of the business has to be given immediately in writing when requested by any supplier, customer or other person with whom the business has dealings.

Companies: The Business Names Act also applies to any company that uses a trading name other than its own, eg if "ABC Foods (XYZ) Ltd" wishes to trade simply as "ABC Foods". In addition, the Companies Act requires a company to paint or affix its name on the *outside* of every office or place where it carries on business.

See also the free Companies House booklet "Choosing a Company Name".

Note there are special rules for Welsh companies.

LICENCES/REGISTRATION

You can start most businesses right away as there is usually no need for licensing or registration. BUT there are exceptions, examples being: selling liquor; providing driving instruction; operating an employment agency; dealing with scrap metal; providing public entertainment; dealing in second-hand goods (including cars); operating as a street trader or mobile shop; driving a taxi or private hire car; operating certain goods and passenger vehicles; cleaning windows; hairdressing; child minding; selling door-to-door; most activities relating to pets or animals; providing credit services (see the "Consumer

Credit Act" on page 26). If you are going to sell or handle food you must speak to the Environmental Health Department at a very early stage of the project (and before you start trading).

Important: The list above is only a sample and failure to obtain a licence or register may be a criminal offence.

KEY POINT Contact your local Council or business advisers to find out if you need to register or get a licence or other approval.

INSURANCES

Where applicable, it is a legal requirement to have vehicle insurance, certain engineering insurances and employers liability insurance. It would be prudent to be adequately insured for other risks so you should discuss your proposed venture with an insurance broker (who should be a registered broker).

The broker may only be able to give you an estimate at this early stage as you probably will not have the full details they require. The various types of insurance which you may consider are covered below:

Employers Liability This is a legal requirement only if you employ some one and then the certificate has to be prominently displayed at the place of work. It is not required by sole-traders (or partnerships) with no employees. This insurance is to protect employers against claims for damages, brought by employees for death or bodily injury sustained in the course of employment (which includes injury caused by other employees for whom you are liable).

Public Liability This provides you with protection against claims for which you may be legally liable, brought by anyone other than employees, for bodily injury or loss or damage to property arising in the course of your business. You should consider this particular insurance cover if customers are likely to visit your home. It also covers the legal costs incurred when defending such claims.

Product Liability This provides protection for legal liability for claims arising from injury, loss or damage due to products you have sold, supplied, repaired, serviced or tested. It can be expensive.

Professional Indemnity This is for anyone who wants to start a business as a consultant (legal, management, technical, marketing, financial etc). This insurance protects you against your legal liability to compensate third parties who have sustained some injury, loss or damage due to your own professional negligence or that of your employees.

Vehicles You must, of course, carry motor insurance but if you intend to use your car or van in the business,

---

PARTICULARS OF OWNERSHIP
of

B R O W N ' S   B & B

as required by the Business Names Act 1985

Full Name(s) of Owner(s)	Address at which Documents can be served
Miss Jean Brown	12, Nosuch Crescent London SW1 1ZZ

An example of a sign, completed with fictitious particulars

Making it Legal

check that your insurance covers you (and any other driver) for the commercial purpose you propose. Generally for a car there will be an additional premium for using it in connection with your business.

Goods In Transit As a rule, motor insurance policies do not cover goods being carried in the vehicle so if you intend to carry goods you may need this additional insurance cover.

Property You may find that your normal buildings insurance is not valid if you operate a business from home, unless you notify the insurers, in writing, and have their full agreement.

Stock, Fixtures & Fittings, Plant and Machinery Certain types of business may be regarded as more risky to an insurer and this will affect your premium. Your insurers may also insist you upgrade the physical security of your home by installing better locks and possibly a burglar alarm.

Be careful not to under-estimate the value of your stock and equipment. Note that if your cover is for "reinstatement value" it provides for the full replacement cost while "indemnity value" is the current market value less the depreciation (which can be significant!). Insurance should cover losses due to theft, vandalism, fire, flood etc. "All risks" (ie accidental damage) can also be arranged in most cases if you require that cover.

Money If your business involves handling cash in significant amounts then insurance cover against theft would be prudent. Policies normally cover loss of money in the premises and also money in transit to or from the bank. If covered for cash in transit be sure to comply with the small print.

Not all insurers will consider taking on home-based businesses, but two who have specific policies are the London & Edinburgh Insurance Co Ltd's "Home-Work" policy (available through most insurance brokers, or tel: 0345 336611) and Tolson Messenger Ltd of 148 King St, London W6 0QU (tel: 0800 374246).

Finally, remember that the services of an insurance broker are free as he or she is paid commission by the insurance companies. A good broker will not try to sell you insurance you do not require but at the same time will be concerned that you do not under-insure. It is a balancing act to a certain extent as you should take out as much insurance as you need, but no more and no less – and in any event you must review the position at least once a year to take into account changes in your business.

KEY POINT Always take the time to read and try to understand your insurance policies.

LEGISLATION

There are many laws that may affect you when you run a business. Here is a brief guide to just some of the more important ones (listed in alphabetical order). Other laws are mentioned elsewhere in this book, in the appropriate chapters. Be sure to consult a solicitor to find out all the laws and regulations that may apply to your own business.

Letterheads There are a number of legal requirements with the information you give on your letterhead. These are illustrated on the opposite page.

Consumer Credit Act In most cases if you are going to provide credit, arrange

credit or HP or if you are going to hire equipment for more than 3 months, then you are likely to need a licence under this Act.

You may not need a licence if, for instance, you are simply accepting payment by credit card or you are simply allowing customers to pay their bills at the end of the week, month or whatever period you work to (this includes normal "trade" credit).

The Act is complex and it is a criminal offence to give credit without a licence unless the exceptions such as mentioned above apply. Contact your local Trading Standards Department for more information.

Consumer Protection Act This Act's main functions are to ensure the safety of goods sold and it also makes it a criminal offence to give consumers a misleading price indication about goods or services. Contact your local Trading Standards Department for more information.

Data Protection Act If you are going to keep information about people on a computer, even if it is just names and addresses, then you usually need to register and pay a fee. For more information contact the Registrar's Enquiry Service on tel: 01625 545745.

Employing Staff If you need to employ someone, then you need to be aware that there are many laws and regulations which apply. Taking on anyone, even part-time, is *not* a decision to take lightly.

FURTHER READING Employing Staff is covered more in *The Greatest Little Business Book* (see the end of this book for ordering details).

BROWN'S B&B

12 Nosuch Crescent
London
SW1 1ZZ

Tel: 0171 123 456

The Best Bed and Breakfast Place In Town
Proprietor: Jean Brown

The Quick Guide to Letterheads

For a **Sole Trader** or **Partnership**, the example (left) shows the three legal requirements for a letterhead: a) business name, b) the name of the sole trader (or partners) and c) for each person named an address at which "documents can be served". Optional features shown here: a sales message, envelope fold line (on the left hand edge) and dots to place an address when using window envelopes.

ABC Foods (XYZ) Ltd

15, Nowhere Place
Edinburgh EH1 1ZZ

Tel: 0131-123 456
Fax: 0131-234 567

Registered in Scotland. Registration Number: 0000
Registered Office: Capital House, King James Square, Edinburgh EH1 1ZZ

For a **Limited Company**, the example (right) shows the four legal requirements for a letterhead: 1) full company name with Limited or Ltd; 2) country of registration; 3) registration number and 4) the registered office address (which may be different to the trading address). Note that if you choose to add Directors' names, then all names must be given.

(Note: These are both fictitious businesses).

Due to space limitations, we have not tried to show a clever design of letterhead or the use of logos etc.

Making it Legal

Financial Services Act This Act requires any person involved in the provision of financial advice, or related services, to register.

Food Safety Act & other Regulations There are stringent rules regarding most aspects of handling, preparing and selling food. For instance, equipment, premises, food handlers, storage, working methods, labelling etc are all covered. Speak to your local Environmental Health Department at the very start of your project.

Trade Descriptions Act This Act requires traders to use correct descriptions of their goods and services.

Unfair Terms In Consumer Contracts Regulations This applies to all terms in a contract (including pre-printed terms on order forms and invoices) where you are supplying goods or services to a consumer. "Small print" that is deemed unfair will not be binding.

Weights & Measures Act This Act applies to anyone selling foods, drinks, toilet preparations etc.

Remember: These are just some of the general laws and regulations that may affect you but you need to know all those that affect your specific business. Many trades and industries have regulations that apply specifically to them.

PROPERTY PROBLEMS

Working from home is obviously the cheapest and simplest way for many businesses to start, and it is becoming very popular, but there are legal constraints. In particular if you live in a council-owned house it will almost certainly be a breach of your tenancy agreement to conduct any business from the house. A few discreet enquiries at your local government offices would let you know where you stand. If you rent privately, it is also likely to be against the rules of your tenancy agreement.

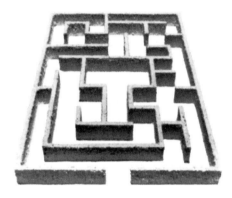

The rules and regulations surrounding the use of your home for a business is confusing to the layman and you need professional guidance to avoid being lost in the maze! Even if you own your home it may be an infringement of local planning regulations or bylaws to work from home. Again, a few discreet enquiries will let you know where you stand. There may also be a restriction imposed in your title deeds.

If you have a mortgage the Building Society or Bank may not like your home being used for your business.

If your neighbours object to your business activities, you could have a problem. So these matters all need very careful consideration and good legal advice at the outset. Also, remember to ask your accountant about the risk of attracting Capital Gains Tax if and when you sell your home.

However, the simple truth is that many businesses operate quite happily from homes (or domestic garages) maintaining a very low profile – minimal advertising (or only using a telephone number on adverts), no advertising signs, no noise, no queues of visiting customers or suppliers . . . Be careful though about potential fire risks (such as welding) because you may discover, too late, that your domestic insurance does not cover that sort of risk!

Working from home is sometimes a short-term situation until a business gets established and moves into commercial premises. Important exceptions are certain office-type activities and businesses (such as painting & decorating) where the home is merely a base.

Business Rates If you have a trade or business sign outside your home or you set aside a room or your garage *exclusively* for business use, then you may be liable for Business Rates on that room (or garage). If there is continued domestic use of that room (or garage) then business rates are not usually applicable, but do get professional advice at an early stage.

TAX & VAT

First, get a copy of the free government leaflet CWL1, titled *Starting your own business?* as it tells you what to do and includes the forms you need.

Inland Revenue (Tax & PAYE) As a sole trader or partner you do not pay PAYE (Pay-As-You-Earn) income tax, which employees have to pay. Instead you pay income tax on the profits of the business.

KEY POINT When you start trading you must notify your local Tax Office without delay.

Notify the Tax Office using the form CWF1, which is provided inside the leaflet CWL1 mentioned on the previous page.

If you are going to employ people, you have to operate PAYE. Remember that if you are a limited company with salaried Directors you will also have to operate PAYE. Contact your local Tax Office (look under "Inland Revenue" in the Phone Book) and ask for a "New Employers Starter Pack".

KEY POINT If you employ anyone or you have salaried Directors, then you must contact your Tax Office without delay.

National Insurance As a sole trader or partner you will normally have to pay a regular Class 2 contribution and your business will in addition have to pay a Class 4 contribution if your profits exceed a certain figure. If your self-employed earnings are likely to be small, you can apply to your local Contributions Agency (DSS) office for a "Small Earnings Exception". (For the current tax rates, see the **Tax Data Page** at the end of this book).

If you are at present in work as an employee paying a Class 1 National Insurance stamp, then if you start a business you will normally have to pay a Class 2 stamp in addition (unless your self-employed earnings are less than the Small Earnings Exception).

KEY POINT When you start trading as a sole trader or partnership notify the DSS without delay.

Visit your local Contributions Agency (DSS) office and ask for copies of their leaflets on self-employment. You could also use this opportunity to discuss how your proposed business will affect any social security benefits you may be receiving.

You can elect to pay your Class 2 contributions monthly direct from your business bank account, but you should not complete the direct debit mandate until you have actually started your business, i.e. do it only when you are committed.

If you form a limited company, as a paid Director you will normally need to pay Class 1 contributions, not Class 2. In addition, the company has to pay an "employer's National Insurance contribution". These are both payable to the Inland Revenue along with your PAYE.

Customs & Excise (VAT) Value Added Tax (VAT) is a tax on most business transactions, including importing goods and some imported services. With few exceptions you will need to register for VAT if, at the end of any month, the total value of the "taxable supplies" you have made in the past 12 months exceeds the VAT registration threshold. For the current threshold figure, see the **Tax Data Page** at the end of this book.

If you exceed the threshold prior to completing your first 12 months in business, then you need to register for VAT immediately. Registration is also required if at any time there are reasonable grounds for believing that the value of the taxable supplies you will make in the next 30 days will exceed the threshold.

"Taxable supplies" are all your sales (other than those that are "exempt supplies", as described overpage).

". . . . You can find Customs & Excise in the Phone Book"

Making it Legal

For VAT purposes, all business transactions come under one of three categories:

Exempt Supplies   This applies to only those very few types of business transaction which are specified as "exempt" from VAT. No VAT is payable and you cannot be VAT registered if you only make exempt supplies.

Zero Rated   This applies to only those types of business which are specified as "zero-rated" for VAT. The current list of zero-rated goods (which may change at any time) includes: young children's clothing and footwear, books, newspapers, public transport and basic foodstuffs (but not catering). No VAT is payable. If your turnover exceeds the threshold, you need to register and then you can recover any VAT on business expenses but there is no need to add VAT to your sales (as they are zero-rated). You could instead choose to apply for exemption from registration if your taxable supplies are mainly or wholly zero-rated.

Standard Rated   This rate applies to almost all other business transactions. If your business is in this category and your turnover has exceeded or is likely to exceed the VAT threshold, you must register for VAT and then add VAT to your prices. But you can then recover VAT you are charged by suppliers.

KEY POINT   If your turnover rises to the VAT registration level, then you must contact Customs & Excise without delay.

To register for VAT, contact your local Customs & Excise VAT Office. See under "Customs & Excise" in the Phone Book. Refer also to the two chapters **Simple Book-keeping** and **Coping with Taxation**.

VAT is a complex tax, but the free booklet available from HM Customs & Excise "Should I Be Registered for VAT?" is easy to read and essential reading for any business. It also includes a VAT Registration Application Form and notes on how to complete the form ∎

Preparing a Mini Business Plan

W HEN you think you have found the idea that will make you lots of money, it is not good enough to simply launch into business without further planning. Now is the time to prepare a mini business plan.

A business plan is just a document which sets out in words and figures the proposed business venture. A good saying is that *"people do not plan to fail they fail to plan"*. Another saying is *"planning is not just the main thing, it is everything"*. Certainly, if you are risking your money, your future and your peace of mind, you will want to know exactly what you are doing. The main benefits of planning are:

● It makes you look objectively at what you intend to do, which is a good discipline in itself.

● It makes you think about not only what is essential for your immediate survival but also for the next six months (preferably a year) ahead.

● It gives you a means to communicate your ideas to others such as the bank manager and accountant.

● It encourages you to make a personal commitment to achieving your goals.

● It provides you with a game plan, which can help you with your decisions as the year progresses.

● It cuts down the number of unpleasant surprises!

There is a great deal of evidence that the prospects of business survival are greatly increased by knowing exactly what you are trying to achieve and how you intend to do it.

Do not give in to the temptation to put planning in the "too-hard-to-do" basket.

It is easy in many cases to argue that the business you are hoping to start is too uncertain for any worthwhile plans to be made but this is seldom true. You may also try to argue that your proposed venture is too small for it to merit a formal business plan, but you may not be so sure if it starts losing money due to inadequate planning.

You should not treat your business plan as a strait-jacket, but neither should you move away from it without having a good reason and a revised plan.

Five Good Tips . . . . . .

When preparing (and later using) your business plan you should keep the following 5 points in mind:

1. Put the plan in writing It is amazing how writing it down removes the fuzziness in your mind and how a lack of detailed planning soon becomes obvious. A written plan also makes it easier to see contradictions and inconsistencies. The financial part of the plan should reveal any funding problems.

2. Keep the plan short In this book we propose a Mini Business Plan which should be adequate for most purposes. If however your home-based business is complex or requires a lot of funding then a more detailed (and lengthy) business plan will be required. How

FURTHER READING

such a plan is produced is covered in **The Greatest Little Business Book** (see the end of this book for ordering details).

3. Plan 6 - 12 months at a time When a small home-based business is started there are sufficient uncertainties to make planning beyond the first year rather meaningless. This does not mean that you wait until the end of the

first year to make a new plan for the second year. Every three months or so you should review the plan and add another three months to it, so it keeps rolling along.

4. Discuss the plan with your advisers Let your accountant and your bank manager look at the plan and listen to their comments. However, if they suggest changes, do not simply accept them without question.

5. Try to stick to the plan Only revise your plan if you discover there is some error or oversight in the assumptions or strategy in the original plan or if there is some new factor beyond your control. Be honest with yourself and, if the change is being made because of lack of effort to reach the targets or something else which is really within your own control, don't change your plan – change your attitude.

THE MINI BUSINESS PLAN

A business plan for a major corporate venture can be a bulky document running to many pages. But it is most unlikely that your home-based venture really needs such a tome.

Probably all you need is a simple document in three parts, as follows:

Part 1 – Project Description.

Part 2 – List of Start-up Costs.

Part 3 – Cashflow Forecast.

The following pages are a "fill-in-the-blanks" Mini Business Plan. You could photocopy it or type it out yourself – it should be possible to type this Plan on only three A4 pages (as this book is smaller than A4 it takes 5 pages here). On page 37 and subsequent pages are Notes to help you.

MINI BUSINESS PLAN   Part 1: Project Description

Your Name	

Your Address	
Tel:	

Describe your business idea	

Proposed Business Name[1]	

What is your (relevant) business experience and qualifications?	

Why is the business suitable for being home-based?	

What do you hope to achieve with your business?[2]	

What are the key factors for success?[3]	

STRENGTHS & WEAKNESSES

What are the likely Strengths of the business?[4]	

What are the likely Weaknesses of the business?[5]	

What are the likely Opportunities for the business?[6]	

What are the potential Threats to the business?[7]	

MARKETING ASPECTS

Who will be your likely customers?[8]	

What is the potential size of the market that you can reach?[9]	

Please refer to the Notes on page 37

MARKETING ASPECTS (continued)

Who is your competition and how strong are they?[10]	
Who are your main suppliers?[11]	
What prices will you charge?[12]	
How will you advertise and promote your business?[13]	

LEGAL ASPECTS

| Are there any problems in working from your home?[14] | |
| Does your proposed business need any licence?[15] | |

FINANCIAL ASPECTS

| How much start-up money is needed? (This is the **Grand Total** on page 35) | £ |

| What is your estimate of 1st year sales? (This should relate to Line 1 of the page 36 Cashflow) | £ |

From where do you propose getting the start-up money?	Yourself	£
	Bank	£
	Other	£
	Other	£

Financial Notes:

TIME & ACTION PLAN

When do you propose to start the business?	
How will your time be divided amongst the various aspects of your business and the rest of your life?	
What are the next two tasks you need to do?	1.
	2.

Please refer to the Notes on page 37

MINI BUSINESS PLAN   Part 2: Start-Up Costs

CAPITAL EXPENDITURE (& Related Items)

	Details	Costs[16]
Office Equipment (eg computer, software, fax, copier, answering machine)		£
		£
		£
		£
		£
Furniture (eg desk, workbench, shelving)		£
		£
		£
		£
Machinery & Tools		£
		£
Vehicle (incl. tax & insurance)		£
		£
Other Items (eg changes to home)		£
		£
		£

ADMINISTRATION SET-UP COSTS

	Details	
Accountant's Fees		£
Legal Fees		£
Licences		£
		£
Letterheads & Business Cards		£
		£
Stationery (eg paper, pens, accounts book)		£
		£
		£
Business Insurances		£
	Sub-total	£

Please refer to the Notes on page 37

STOCK or RAW MATERIALS[17]

Suppliers	Details	Costs[16]
		£
		£
		£
		£
		£
		£
		£
		£
		£
		£
		£

ADVERTISING & PROMOTION

	Details	
Advertising Plan (for first 3 months)		£
		£
Exterior Signs		£
Press Releases		£
Leaflets		£
Other Promotions		£
		£

OTHER COSTS (Not Already Covered)

Item	Details	
		£
		£
		£
	Sub-Total	£
	Sub-Total from p34	£
	Contingency[18]	£
	Grand Total	**£**

Please refer to the Notes on page 37

MINI BUSINESS PLAN Part 3: Simplified 6-Month Cashflow Forecast

		Month 1	Month 2	Month 3	Month 4	Month 5	Month 6	TOTALS
	CASH IN							
1	**Takings (i.e. Sales)**							
2	**Bank (or other) Loans**							
3	**Owner's Capital**							
4	**Other Money (eg Grants)**							
5	**TOTAL CASH IN**							
	CASH OUT							
6	**CAPITAL EXPENDITURE**							
7	**ADMIN. SET-UP COSTS**							
8	**STOCK/RAW MATERIALS**							
9	**ADVERTS & PROMOTION**							
10	**Bank Charges/Interest**							
11	**Drawings/Salaries/Nat.Ins.**							
12	**Electric/Gas/Heat**							
13	**HP/Lease/Loan Payments**							
14	**Motor Expenses**							
15	**Postage/Parcels**							
16	**Repairs & Maintenance**							
17	**Staff Wages & PAYE**							
18	**Stationery/Printing**							
19	**Sundries**							
20	**Telephone/Fax**							
21	**Travelling**							
22	**VAT (if VAT-registered)**							
23	**Other Expenses**							
24	**TOTAL CASH OUT**							
25	**Net Cashflow**							
26	**Opening Balance**							
27	**CLOSING BALANCE**							

Please refer to the Notes on page 38

MINI BUSINESS PLAN   Notes to help you complete your Plan

Note 1. **Proposed Business Name.** *Remember the requirements of the Business Names Act mentioned in the previous chapter.*

Note 2. **What do you hope to achieve with your business?** *Is this a part-time or full-time venture? Do you see it as temporary or permanent? Do you hope the business will grow or will you be satisfied with it remaining small?*

Note 3. **What are the key factors for success?** *There are usually one or two factors which will be critical to the success of your proposed business. What are they?*

Note 4. **What are the likely Strengths of the business?** *The strengths could arise, for example, out of your personal strengths or the advantages of being small and operating from home.*

Note 5. **What are the likely Weaknesses of the business?** *The weaknesses may arise from your personal short-comings (such as a lack of sales experience), or the small size of your business (which may have a limited range of goods or services to sell). Be honest with yourself when answering this question.*

Note 6. **What are the likely Opportunities for the business?** *Many of your opportunities arise out of the weaknesses of your competition, but do not forget that their opportunities also arise out of your weaknesses! Are your competitors too expensive? Are they difficult to do business with? Are they badly located? Do they provide a poor service to customers?*

Note 7. **What are the potential Threats to the business?** *The threats to your business may not all be obvious. Think about all the things that could go wrong (just about everything!). You will have "external threats", i.e. factors outside the business and outwith your control, such as changes in legislation. There are also "internal threats", i.e. factors within the business which ought to be under your control, such as problems in finding skilled help, production problems, difficulty in meeting demand etc.. Other threats include: changes in taste and fashion; new competition; price cutting by competitors; recession; fire or burglary in your house; personal illness; domestic upheaval. You should make contingency plans to meet these threats and any others you can think of.*

Note 8. **Who will be your likely customers?** *This needs careful thought. Put yourself in the shoes of likely customers. What are you offering that will attract them? Remember that they are surviving without you at the present time.*

Note 9. **What is the potential size of the market that you can reach?** *Be realistic. You will probably only be able to make sales to a tiny proportion of the potential market, but will that be enough to sustain your business?*

Note 10. **Who is your competition and how strong are they?** *Strong competitors will not simply stand back and let you muscle into their territory. They will probably counter-attack, so you need to consider this matter carefully.*

Note 11. **Who are your main suppliers?** *If you are selling or using a product, any supplier problems can quickly cripple your business. Have you contacted suitable suppliers? Are you confident in their ability to supply what you need (and on time!)? Do you know their prices and trading terms? Note: Many businesses complain about poor suppliers.*

Note 12. **What prices will you charge?** *First, please refer to the next chapter in this book.*

Note 13. **How will you advertise and promote your business?** *First, please refer to the next chapter, then summarise here what you plan to do.*

Note 14. **Are there any legal problems in working from your home?** *Have you spoken to a solicitor?*

Note 15. **Does your proposed business need any licence?** *Have you spoken to the relevant authorities?*

Note 16. **Costs.** *If you are not VAT-registered, include any VAT that you are charged.*

Note 17. **Stock/Raw Materials.** *This is just your start-up stock as the cashflow forecast covers replacement stock/raw materials.*

Note 18. **Contingency.** *This is for all the things you forgot to add and for unexpected things that can (and usually do) crop up. Allow a contingency of 10% to 50%, depending on how sure you are with your figures.*

MINI BUSINESS PLAN   Notes to help you complete your Plan

		Month 1	Month 2	Month 3
	CASH IN	May	June	July
1	Takings (i.e. Sales)	400	800	1000
2	Bank (or other) Loans			
3	Owner's Capital	1500		
4	Other Money (eg Grants)			
5	TOTAL CASH IN	1900	800	1000
	CASH OUT			
6	CAPITAL EXPENDITURE	750	140	
7	ADMIN. SET-UP COSTS	800	100	
8	STOCK/RAW MATERIALS			
9	ADVERTS & PROMOTION	200	200	200
10	Bank Charges/Interest			
11	Drawings/Salaries/Nat.Ins.	300	400	400
12	Electric/Gas/Heat			
13	HP/Lease/Loan Payments			
14	Motor Expenses			
15	Postage/Parcels	110	60	60
16	Repairs & Maintenance			
17	Staff Wages & PAYE			
18	Stationery/Printing	90		
19	Sundries	100	50	40
20	Telephone/Fax	250		
21	Travelling	70	20	40
22	VAT (if VAT-registered)			
23	Other Expenses			
24	TOTAL CASH OUT	2670	970	740
25	Net Cashflow	(770)	(170)	260
26	Opening Balance	0	(770)	(940)
27	CLOSING BALANCE	(770)	(940)	(680)

What Is A Cashflow Forecast?

If you have never done a Cashflow Forecast before then you may be forgiven for thinking it is just something else to waste your valuable time and only relevant to "big business", but this is not so. One of the most common reasons a business gets into financial trouble is due to "cashflow problems". This usually occurs when goods (or services) are bought on credit and later when the bills come in there is no money (or overdraft facility) to meet those bills. Cashflow problems may also result from the business having too little work or suffering from bad payers.

In every business, cash comes in . . . . . but so do the bills and it can soon become difficult to control. This is where a Cashflow Forecast is useful as it helps you to forecast your future cash requirements and any problems can be spotted early and something done about it.

How Does It Work?

A Cashflow Forecast is just that – a forecast of the cash (i.e. all the money) flowing in and out of the business for the months ahead. At this stage you may be saying "that's impossible", but it can be done with sufficient accuracy to make the effort worthwhile. And it will take a bit of effort to complete, particularly if your business is new and some of your figures are little better than good guesses.

Most businesses (new or established) will find the CASH OUT figures are straightforward to estimate. But a new business will find line 1 difficult to predict. In that case you can do a "break-even" cashflow where you complete the form leaving line 1 to the very end and then you insert what sales you need to at least keep the bottom line 27 positive or within your overdraft limit.

Worked Example

The worked example (left) shows the forecast for the first 3 months trading of a small service business. The vertical columns are in months. In this example, to start the business the owner is providing £1500 capital and there is a bank

Preparing a Mini Business Plan

overdraft facility of £1000. (Note: The figures at the foot of the cashflow opposite are in brackets to indicate they are negative, i.e. the bank account is in overdraft).

In the example, as the business is new, the "Opening Balance" on line 26 is zero.

Doing Your Own Cashflow Forecast

Two points before you start . . . (1) as any prediction becomes more hazy as you look further into the future, you may prefer to try forecasting only 2-3 months ahead at a time rather than 6 months or even a year; (2) a golden rule with Cashflow Forecasts is to be pessimistic. In particular, don't over-estimate likely sales or under-estimate overheads which always seem to get larger than expected.

Method

1. Enter the months across the top.

2. Omit £ signs, exclude pence, and round the figures up or down (eg £19.68 becomes simply 20 in a cashflow).

3. Work in pencil, since (a) you will probably need to make several attempts to complete the form and (b) when you have completed the first month's trading you can rub out that column's pencil figures and insert the actual figures in ink. You can then see *actual* from *forecast*.

4. The *actual* figures will come from your Accounts Book.

5. If you are offering credit, as this is a forecast of *cash* flow, then you show the "Sales" in the month when you expect to receive the money, not in the month when you invoice your customers.

6. Now do line 1 for the whole form (unless you are doing a "break-even" cashflow in which case this is done last).

7. Complete lines 2 to 4 for the *first* month then put the total of lines 1 to 4 in line 5. *Note:* To distinguish between money made from sales and money from loans or your own capital, you might move lines 2 to 4 to *below* line 25, so the "Net Cashflow" then reflects the actual trading position.

8. When you have completed lines 6 to 23 for the first month, then total up on line 24 to get the total cash out during that month.

9. Next subtract line 24 from line 5 to get the "Net Cashflow" on line 25.

10. Finally add lines 25 and 26 to get the "Closing Balance" for that first column.

11. This "Closing Balance" becomes the "Opening Balance" for the next column.

12. Repeat steps 7 to 11 for month two.

KEY POINT Never confuse cash *inflow* with *profitability* and note the bottom line of a Cashflow Forecast doesn't represent a "profit" or a "loss".

VAT If you are not registered for VAT, then just ignore line 22 in the Cashflow Forecast. But if you are registered for VAT then you have two options: 1) You can either enter all figures as VAT inclusive and use line 22 just to record the VAT payments you need to make to HM Customs & Excise or 2) You can show the CASH OUT amounts as net of

VAT and put the monthly VAT total in line 22. This second approach makes it easier to reconcile the Cashflow with your accounts records which will be net of VAT.

RAISING THE FINANCE

If you don't need to borrow any money, that's fine, but do check with your local Business Link (in England), Enterprise Agency or T.E.C. (L.E.C. in Scotland) to see if there are any grants available. Some grants need to be applied for before you take any step to start your business or you are automatically disqualified! Don't be disappointed if there are no grants!

The main sources of finance for a small home-based business are:
(1) Yourself; (2) Friends and Relatives, and (3) Banks. If borrowing from friends or relatives, avoid friction by putting your loan agreement in writing.

A bank will probably be your main source of outside funds. Remember that banks do not like to lend more than about half the total cost of the venture. Bank borrowing is usually in two forms – loans and overdrafts.

Bank Loans & Overdrafts Loans are made normally to finance Capital

Preparing a Mini Business Plan

Expenditure (i.e. computers, equipment and vehicles). These loans can be at either fixed or variable rates of interest and are repaid either monthly or quarterly over a pre-agreed "term", usually 2 to 5+ years.

In contrast, overdrafts are for short-term working capital. This can bridge the gap between: a) buying stock and reselling it; b) providing a service (particularly to trade customers) and waiting to be paid; or c) buying raw materials and later selling the made-up product.

An overdraft, if granted, will be for an agreed amount. *Never* exceed this limit without prior permission from the bank manager, because the facility can be withdrawn at any time if the bank thinks you are mishandling your financial affairs.

An overdraft is usually the cheapest money you can borrow as you only pay interest on the daily balance "in the red", this interest usually having to be repaid quarterly.

Many businesses, even very small ones, use a combination of loan and overdraft facilities when they start and to run their ventures.

All banks publish and display their "Base Lending Rate" – as a small business you will normally pay several per cent more for your loan or overdraft. Ensure you know what rate you are going to be charged and remember it is usually negotiable!

Security   Banks often require some form of security and will often request your home as security (if you own it).

Where the market value of the house (less any outstanding mortgage) is substantial in comparison to the size of loan requested, then a home can provide useful and non-onerous security. Where this is not the case then it is best not offered nor accepted for security due to the unnecessary additional risk taken by the entrepreneur and family.

KEY POINT

If you offer your home as security, the bank is able to repossess your home if your business fails to pay its debts ∎

YOU do not have a business unless you can make *sales* and in most cases you need to make a lot of sales just to break-even financially. To achieve this requires four things:

● A Saleable Product (or Service)
● Correct Pricing
● Targeted Advertising/Promotion
● Good Selling Technique

We shall look at each of these four factors in turn.

A SALEABLE PRODUCT (or SERVICE)

To make reasonable sales you must have a product (or a service) which people actually *want!* This may sound obvious but a surprising number of businesses run into problems simply because there is insufficient demand for what they are trying to sell. No amount of clever advertising, catchy promotions, juggling with prices or smart selling can rectify such a basic fault.

If what you are offering is innovative then the risk is greatest, though the potential rewards are also greatest. When a large company launches an innovative product they

"When she said she was a sculptor, I thought bird baths or something."

put a great deal of effort (and money) behind its launch. You will see it on TV and in the papers. But even investing millions does not guarantee success as many have discovered and you are unlikely to have such funds available for your launch.

A safer path to tread is to offer a better version of what people are already buying so you know there is a *demand* for it. If you are selling a product, "better" could mean technically superior or having more features, or just be easier to use. If you are offering a service then there may be plenty of scope for you to be better than your competitors by more thoughtful handling of your customers. Whatever the type of business, "better" could mean a better standard of service (many businesses in this country still treat their customers poorly).

If you think you are offering a better version of what people are already buying then it follows that you must have competitors. You should ask yourself "why should anyone change over to using me and how will they know mine is better?"

Most people think their business idea is great and will soon make them a fortune or at the very worst will make them a living. Unfortunately too few people seem to be able to do a rational assessment of the viability of their proposed business idea. This is where the advice of a third party such as a business counsellor from your local Business Link (in England), Enterprise Agency or T.E.C. (L.E.C. in Scotland) can prove invaluable. Some good market research should also help you to avoid making a big mistake.

CORRECT PRICING

Too few businesses do their pricing properly, because it is not easy, especially if you are new to business. First, the meanings of some important terms:

"Overheads" (or "Fixed Costs") refers to business expenditure which is basically constant, i.e. "fixed", irrespective of the level of trading, eg your business insurance.

"Direct Costs" (or "Variable Costs") refers to business expenditure which varies directly in relation to the level of business, eg the costs of raw materials or stock.

"Mark-up" $\text{Mark-up} = \dfrac{(\text{selling price} - \text{cost price})}{\text{cost price}} \times 100\%$

"Margin" $\text{Margin} = \dfrac{(\text{selling price} - \text{cost price})}{\text{selling price}} \times 100\%$

How to get Sales

PRICING A PRODUCT

A straightforward way to price a product is as follows:

1. If you are working alone, making things:

Selling price/unit =
(cost of raw material + your wages + overheads contribution) + mark-up + VAT

Cost of raw material: This should be relatively easy to work out, but remember to allow for wastage. *Your Wages:* Work out what wages you need to take from the business each week to meet your domestic bills then divide this by the total number of items you can make in a week. *Overheads Contribution:* This is the total weekly overheads of the business divided by the number of items made each week. *Mark-up:* The mark-up is a small surplus (say 10-20%) to provide funds for new product development or simply to save against any future contingencies. *VAT:* This is only added if you are VAT-registered and the product itself is VAT rated.

An important aspect of this simplified costing method is that it assumes your rate of sales matches your production, i.e. you are selling everything almost as fast as you can make them. If not, then the figures become nonsense.

KEY POINT Be cautious about pricing your product on the assumption that you will be operating at full production all the time for that is most unlikely.

Example: Assume you are self-employed making either small craft products, garments or whatever. Assume also the raw materials cost £10/unit and each item takes 1 hour to make, so in a 40 hour week you could make 40 such items. Assume you need to draw £150 per week from the business to support your domestic expenses and assume your business overheads (business insurance, essential travel etc) come to £60 per week. Then (assuming no wastage):

Selling price/unit = (£10 + £3.75 + £1.50) + 10% = £16.78

You might consider selling at £16.99 or £17.50 depending on the competition and what the market can stand.

In this example, the maximum annual turnover (i.e. sales) = 40 x 52 x £17.50 = £36,400 which is below the current VAT threshold so the business would not need to be VAT registered and no VAT should be added to the price.

2. If you are a wholesaler or retailer:

Selling price/unit = net cost price + mark-up + VAT (where applicable)

Example: If, as a retailer, you buy an article for £4.65 net (i.e. without VAT added) and if the typical trade mark-up is 85% then the selling price = £4.65 + 85% + VAT which equals £10.11 (if the VAT rate is 17.5% and you are registered for VAT). There are four points to consider:

1. You may consider selling this article for £9.95 as that sounds more appealing to a customer.
2. Find out the typical retail mark-up percentages for your trade. *Note:* Retail mark-ups vary widely and wholesale mark-ups are generally smaller.
3. Keep your prices in line with your competitors.
4. Check the Cashflow Forecast reflects your mark-ups.

PRICING A SERVICE

The pricing of a service is normally based on hourly labour rates plus material costs. For consultancy or freelance work this is more usually called "fees plus expenses".

Calculating Hourly Labour Rates First of all find out typical "going rates" for what you are planning to do by asking a trade association or people in the trade outside your area who are therefore not likely to be competitors. Next, if you plan to employ anyone, check that you can give them an adequate hourly wage out of that, making allowance for downtime and profit.

Finally, insert that figure into your Cashflow Forecast by assuming you (and any employees) will be productive (i.e. doing work for which you can actually charge) for, say 50% of the working week (the actual figure may be even lower and is unlikely to be much above 75%). By being productive for 50% means that in a typical 40 hour week you will only be charging for 20 hours but having to pay your staff for 40. The remaining 20 unproductive hours are absorbed in getting sales, doing paperwork, travelling, buying materials etc. If the Cashflow Forecast figures look good and your labour rate is about that for the trade then that is a good start.

Materials Some people charge materials "at cost". You should be wary of charging for materials at what you paid for them because there are hidden costs you are ignoring such as the time you take to find and buy the materials, the cost of materials held in stock (i.e. the overdraft charges you may be paying for the stock), the cost of travel to pick up the materials, and so on. Some businesses consider "at cost" being the retail price whereas they purchase the goods wholesale thereby giving themselves some useful margin.

Estimates and Quotations   An "estimate" is the approximate price of something, but usually a buyer will ask for a "quotation" and in writing. A quotation is a fixed price and if agreed is binding on both parties. As all quotations involve a degree of guesswork, you should carefully record your actual expenditure on the contract (by simply noting each day what man-hours and materials were spent on the contract). In this way your guesses should get better with experience.

TARGETED ADVERTISING & PROMOTION

You can have a desirable product or service to sell at an attractive price but if nobody knows about it your business will obviously fail! There are many ways of finding customers and even a small business may need to use a combination of these. Some ways are more costly than others while some are more effective. Unfortunately cost and effect are not always clearly related! The different methods are basically (in approximate order of ascending cost):

Producing Press Releases   This is relatively cheap as all it takes is a letter to each relevant publication (possibly enclosing a sample, or photo, if appropriate). To get the best results requires a bit of research – first to ensure you send your Press Release to suitable publications and second, to get the name of the editor to whom you should send it. A Press Release is typed on your letterhead and describes (very briefly) what you are doing, stressing the newness, topicality and the human element (i.e. a bit about yourself). When writing the Press Release, keep thinking to yourself "Will this be interesting to a reader?"

Although it may be gratifying to your ego to see your name in print, the tangible result (i.e. sales) is very much more difficult to quantify, so don't be too disappointed if an article generates little sales activity.

Issuing Leaflets   This can be quite cheap, unless you are thinking of producing a substantial full colour brochure. Leaflets are a good way of summarising the products or services that you can supply. But before you get engrossed in the design of a leaflet, you need to ask yourself just how you are going to *distribute* them. Distribution is the key. You can post them to people, put them through letterboxes locally, hand them to prospective clients when you meet them or at an exhibition, enclose them (loosely) with a trade publication etc etc. We are all subjected to many, many leaflets so yours will have to battle to catch someone's attention.

To get an idea of cost, visit a local instant printer and talk it through with them. The more colours you add, the more costly it becomes. Beware of printing too many leaflets as you will find that the information soon becomes out of date and you end up with cartons of useless paper.

Doing Special Promotions   It is difficult to generalise about the cost of doing a special promotion as it does rather depend on what you are intending. Such a promotion could consist of getting a group of people together at your home and trying to persuade them to buy what you have to sell (like party plan selling). This is obviously cheap to do. A more expensive version is where you hire a function room in a hotel for your presentation. If you are able to tag onto some other event which gathers potential customers together, so much the better – for instance, you may be able to address a meeting of a trade association or your local Chamber of Commerce (or whatever is appropriate to your business).

Taking a Stand at an Exhibition   This can be quite expensive, particularly if it is a big national trade exhibition, but even the smallest of businesses do exhibit. To check if you should, visit the exhibition and try to talk to businesses similar to your own and then judge if it would be worthwhile. A word of caution – don't be dazzled by the glitter and excitement of big exhibitions. Exhibiting is hard work, needs a great deal of preparation and can be an expensive flop.

Doing regular Advertising   There are many ways of advertising, including direct mailshot letters, cards in shop windows, posters, adverts in directories (eg Yellow Pages), adverts in newspapers and magazines.

Businesses providing local services (such as plumbing, erecting satellite TV aerials or doing building repairs) can advertise successfully using the classified columns in the local press, cards in shop windows or business cards put through letterboxes.

In contrast, businesses which have a wider market (geographically) may find it more difficult to get cost effective advertising. Taking display adverts in publications requires a great deal of knowledge of marketing and advertising to have any hope of getting a satisfactory response.

People tend to suppose that because they had a large half-page advert in a newspaper or magazine backed up with some editorial, now everyone knows about their business – WRONG! It is a sad reality but people forget adverts almost as soon as they have read them. This is *unless* they happen

How to get Sales

to have a need at the *precise* moment they see the advert, so you would probably have to advertise regularly, i.e. weekly (or monthly if it is a monthly publication), but this would soon become very expensive.

With all advertising, be it a card in a shop window or an expensive colour advertisement in a glossy magazine, an important element is correct targeting, i.e. the advert needs to be placed where your potential customers are looking. If this sounds too obvious, just give it a little thought and you will see how others are missing this vital point. It is most unlikely that the whole population is your potential market and so you need to target that small part who are likely customers.

GOOD SELLING TECHNIQUE

You can have a prospective customer but still lose the sale if you handle it wrongly. Worse still you can have a customer who is anxious to buy, almost with the cash in their hand, but still lose the sale! It must be said that people who are setting up a new business and have a *sales background* have a great advantage over those who have never made sales before. One trap you should avoid, if you are inexperienced, is to assume that you can get someone else to do your selling. Very rarely can a new small business attract the right sort of salesperson, "rep" or agent. You must realise that this is *your* business and you are going to have to do the sales *yourself!*

So let's see what is involved. Good selling technique is not about being a pushy salesperson, but it does involve:

● Knowing your products and business thoroughly.

● Understanding your customer's needs.

● Listening carefully to hear what the customer wants.

● Answering the customer's queries honestly.

● Having the courage to follow up and close the sale.

It would be fair to say that you should succeed in selling if you have a genuine empathy for your customers, have the right product or service to offer and at the right price. In time, a good business develops friendly relations with its customers and this will help should a new competitor appear or the business be faced with some other problem.

Using The Telephone Selling by phone is a technique which is of particular use to the small business with limited manpower and where the proprietor often has to do the sales work in addition to running the rest of the business. However, to use the phone effectively requires both skill and practice.

The main uses of the phone in this context are: (1) Cold calling potential customers; (2) As a follow up to a sales letter you have sent and (3) In response to someone contacting you wanting more information or to place an order.

If you are phoning someone, here are some hints . . . .

1. Keep a smile on your face (it shows in your voice).
2. Speak clearly and slowly.
3. As there is no visual contact, it's important to give your name (and business name) at the very start.
4. Explain the purpose of your call.
5. Keep your product/sales information in front of you.
6. Remember the customer will be thinking "What's in this for me?" and may be impatient to get back to what they were doing before you phoned them.
7. Close the sale, or arrange an appointment to see them (whichever is appropriate).
8. Summarise what has been agreed (then perhaps later confirm it in writing).
9. If you can, thank them for their time.

If you plan to make unsolicited calls to consumers, ensure your calls comply with the Office of Fair Trading Guidelines which can be found printed in the BT Phone Books.

FURTHER READING The whole subject of Marketing, Advertising and Selling is covered in depth in the companion book, ***The Greatest Sales & Marketing Book*** (see the end of this book for order details) ■

Simple Book-keeping

THERE are several good reasons why you need to keep a close watch on your business finances. For a start, the Inland Revenue needs to know how much profit you are making so they can tax you. Second, you need to know who owes you money and who you owe money to. And a third reason is you need to control your cashflow so that you always have cash in the bank to meet your bills. People who are successful in business tend to be those who take an interest in the financial side of their operations.

As many people don't know much about keeping accounts when they start in business, they hope their accountant will "do the books" for them. This is not necessarily ideal for two reasons. First, and most importantly, knowing your exact financial position is essential to managing the business and if you or your spouse or partner keeps the books then you ought to know what's going on. Second, using an accountant to do your books will be expensive.

So what do you have to do? It's quite simple really . . . .

1. *Business purchases* – keep the receipts for everything you buy.

2. *Sales* – keep duplicates of all sales invoices you raise.

3. *Written Record* – keep a record of the above transactions plus any others relating to the business finances (eg bank direct debits). Doing this is called book-keeping and is done using an accounts book.

Let's look at this in more detail . . .

Business Purchases You need to keep the receipts for *everything* you buy in connection with your business as proof of those expenses. Despite using

the word "receipt", an "invoice" is usually acceptable. A receipt (or an invoice) should give the supplier's name and address, date, amount and a description of the purchase. Other than for small amounts, it should also give your business name.

Receipts (or invoices) should all be filed in some manner. One suggestion is to divide them into those paid by cheque and those paid by cash. Those paid by cheque should be put in *cheque number* sequence using a 2-hole lever arch file.

Invoices too small to be hole-punched can be stuck onto a larger piece of paper before filing. Write the cheque number on an outside corner of the invoice so that it can be cross-referred to easily.

You can use a card divider in the lever arch file to separate *paid* from *unpaid* invoices. File unpaid invoices on one side of the card, and when you pay them, move them to the other side of the card. This should prevent you from forgetting to pay any bills.

Petty cash receipts (or invoices) could be filed in an envelope, one for each month. Alternatively you could use another lever arch file. Petty cash receipts (or invoices) should be in *date sequence* and numbered sequentially from, say, 001.

Simple Book-keeping

A Record of Sales You should issue an invoice (numbered sequentially) for every sale you make and you must keep a copy. Use your letterhead for an invoice or a duplicate invoice book. You should also record any other income.

Written Records The main record you need to keep is your accounts book, which is a record of all your business financial transactions. You must also retain your business bank statements, pay-in books, cheque book stubs, orders and delivery notes, relevant business correspondence, import and export documents, copies of any credit/debit notes and a list of goods taken from the business for personal use or supplied to someone else in exchange for goods or services. In addition, if you transfer any money between your business and personal bank or building society accounts, then you must also retain those statements or pass books. You must also record all purchases/sales of assets used in your business. At an early stage, ask your accountant what records they will want to see at the end of the year. (*Note 1:* If you employ any staff or make payments to sub-contractors in the construction industry, you will need to keep further records. *Note 2:* If you plan to trade in certain second-hand goods, eg cars, you will need to keep additional VAT records).

VAT If you become registered for VAT, then you need to keep additional records and there are specific requirements as to the information given on all your invoices. In general a VAT invoice (usually called a "tax invoice") should have a unique identifying number and give the supplier's name, address and VAT number, the date the invoice is issued, the type of supply (eg sale or rental), the tax point, a full description and quantity of the goods or services, the rate of cash discount offered (if any), the rate of VAT, the total (excluding VAT), the amount of VAT and the total payable. The invoice should also give the customer's name and address unless you mainly sell direct to the public and the invoice total is under £100.

If selling to other EC countries, your customer's VAT number and country code must also appear on your invoice (in addition to your own VAT number with a GB prefix).

If you think you may need to register for VAT, then read the free publications on VAT from HM Customs & Excise.

BOOK-KEEPING SYSTEMS

Keep It Simple! There are many different ways to keep accounts and almost any way is acceptable provided you, your accountant, the tax inspector (and if you are VAT-registered, the VAT inspector), can all understand it! It is essential you understand the system yourself as some businesses have failed partly because their book-keeping systems were so complex that the proprietors could not understand them.

Single Book or Multi-Ledger? When you start in business you will probably only need to keep a single accounts book, but if your business grows you may need to consider moving to more complex (and expensive) systems. Not surprisingly, operating a multi-ledger system takes much more time as it involves double-entry book-keeping, and its users often ultimately consider computerising their accounts.

Multi-ledger accounts systems are outside the scope of this book as they are of less relevance to a new-start small home-based business.

Single Accounts Book Systems

Every business needs an accounts book to record the funds received and payments being made. It is sometimes referred to as a *Cash Book* .

Accounts books appropriate to the smaller business fall into two categories: (1) those which are pre-printed so the user only has to fill in the figures where directed (eg the example opposite) or (2) "blank" accounts books which are merely ruled with lines and columns but have no headings or instructions and so need some knowledge of book-keeping.

Some Accounts Books on the market:

1. The Best Small Business Accounts Books (*Price about £8.95 from main branches of W.H. Smith or Ryman's or by mail-order from Hingston Publishing See page 119 for ordering details*).

These two accounts books are from the publishers of "The Greatest Guide to Home-based Business" and are intended to be the simplest on the market for non-VAT registered small businesses (page 48 has details of a VAT version).

The books have colour coded covers – the YELLOW BOOK is for a *cash business with mainly daily sales* and is suitable for a wide variety of home-based businesses, such as music teachers, party plan distributors, B&B, home hairdressers, driving instructors, gardeners etc. A page from the YELLOW BOOK is shown opposite (much reduced in size) and there is one such page for each week of the year.

The BLUE BOOK is for a *credit business where sales are mainly invoiced* and is suitable for consultants, freelancers, agents, secretarial service providers, professionals, writers, builders, "handymen", importers and similar businesses. Pages from the BLUE BOOK are shown

The Best Small Business Accounts Books

These books are for non-VAT registered businesses. One book is for a *cash* business and its cover is colour-coded YELLOW. The other book is for a *credit* business and its cover is colour-coded BLUE.

The illustration (right) is a fictitious example given in the YELLOW BOOK. As you can see, all weekly transactions are recorded on one page.

Normally A4 (210 x 297mm) in size the page has been reduced to fit here.

Week 1

commencing **6th May**

MONEY RECORD

	£	p
Money in hand at start of week	178	23

DAILY TAKINGS

	£	p
Monday	63	12
Tuesday	39	73
Wednesday	127	32
Thursday	98	40
Friday	122	43
Saturday	163	82
Sunday		
Total Takings	614	82

OTHER MONEY, LOANS etc

	£	p
Cash from Bank	50	00
From Private a/c	1000	00
Total	1050	00

WEEK'S MONEY BALANCE

	£	p
Money at start of week plus Daily Takings plus Other Money, Loans etc	1843	05
Less Total Bankings	1571	71
Less Cash Payments	161	02
Leaves: **Balance**	110	32

	£	p
Money in hand at end of week	110	22

Discrepancy ±	−	10p

BANK RECORD

	£	p
Bank Balance at start of week	841	27

DAILY BANKINGS

	£	p
Monday	158	23
Tuesday		
Wednesday	80	65
Thursday		
Friday	1332	83
Saturday		
Sunday		
Total Bankings	1571	71

BANK DIRECT DEBITS etc

	£	p
Cashed Cheques	50	00
Charges/Interest	34	75
HP/Lease/Loan		
Total	84	75

WEEK'S BANK BALANCE

	£	p
Bank Balance at start of week plus Daily Bankings less Bank Direct Debits plus Bank Credits	2328	23
Less Chq Payments	1920	21
Leaves: **Balance**	408	02

BANK STATEMENT CHECK

	£	p
Balance (from above)	408	02
Not yet on Statement: Add total cheques	1509	00
Less total bankings	1332	83
Leaves:	584	19

PAYMENTS RECORD

	PAID BY CASH			PAID BY CHEQUE		
	Ref	£	p	Ref	£	p
Stock/Raw Materials						
A. Jones	133	22	20			
A. Supply Co				072	87	23
I.M. Quick	134	12	32			
Brown & Son				073	107	24
J. Smith Ltd				076	156	90
Stock/Raw Materials Sub-Total		34	52		351	37
Advertising/Promotion						
Business Insurances						
Cleaning						
Drawings/Salaries/NI/Pension						
Self	140	80	00			
Electric/Gas/Heat **Elec**				074	23	79
Fees (eg Accountant, Lawyer)						
Motor – Fuel				079	9	00
– Repairs/Service						
– Tax/Insurance						
Postage/Parcels	136	1	12			
Rates						
Rent						
Repairs/Maintenance						
Staff Wages						
B. Good				075	22	60
A. Helper	139	40	00			
Staff PAYE/NI						
Stationery/Printing	137	3	50			
Sundries 135 56p 138 £1.32		1	88			
Telephone/Fax						
Travelling						
Other Expenses						
Refund Customer (by post)				077	13	45
CAPITAL EXPENDITURE						
Van (2nd hand)				078	1500	00
Total Cash & Cheque Payments		161	02		1920	21

© 1991 P Hingston

Simple Book-keeping

on pages 50-52 (reduced in size). There are 4 pages to each month.

The choice of book (i.e. YELLOW or BLUE) depends basically on whether you are handling cash or submitting invoices for payment by cheque.

These accounts books all come with full instructions, worked examples and a special feature of the books is their "self-balancing" columns. These make it much easier to calculate the money and bank balances. At the end of each book are simple summary sheets to complete at the end of the tax year. An accountant would need these in order to complete your Tax Return.

The Best Small Business Accounts Books are suitable for Sole Traders, Partnerships or Limited Companies.

For PC Computer Users:
The Best Small Business Accounts Software *(Available only by mail-order – see page 119 for ordering details).* This software for PCs mimics the non-VAT accounts books, so for the YELLOW BOOK a file represents a week and the screen shows a similar layout to that in the book. Similarly with the BLUE BOOK's monthly pages. The programs are basic so they are easy to understand and you could be up and running in about an hour or so. There are no heavy manuals to wade through and no long learning curve.

This simple software runs on most PCs (not Apple Macs) from a 286 upwards and takes minimal disk space.

2. The Best VAT Business Accounts Book *(Price about £9.95 + VAT from main branches of W.H. Smith, Ryman's or by mail-order from Hingston Publishing – see page 119).*
To complement *The Best Small Business Accounts Books*, there is a self-contained VAT version of the BLUE BOOK. This has a similar format but with additional columns for VAT and a new section to list VAT Inputs and Outputs. There are also sections to record trade with other EC Member States.

The VAT Account has been specially designed to make the completion of VAT Returns much easier.

3. The Simplex D *(Available from most stationers, price about £9.95).* This book is primarily for small non-VAT registered businesses which have transactions, i.e. purchases or sales, almost daily. The book provides one page per week and contains instructions and example specimen pages. There are also end-of-year summary sheets at the rear.

If using a Simplex D and your business grows and you need to register for VAT then you can use their "Simplex VAT Record Book" in conjunction with the Simplex D.

4. Collins Self-employed Account Book *(Available from most stationers, price about £17).* Designed for VAT-registered traders, it contains instructions and example specimen pages. The book also has sections to permit you to calculate and record your VAT.

5. Twinlock Complete Accounts Book *(Available from most stationers, price about £16).* This is an accounts book suitable for many VAT-registered businesses. It is a loose-leaf binder style of book which has the advantage that you can add sheets. It has instructions and worked examples.

Blank Heading, Ruled Accounts Books
All the pre-printed books mentioned above can be used by almost anyone without book-keeping experience (with a little coaching from their accountant or business counsellor). In contrast, the blank heading, ruled type of accounts book requires someone with suitable book-keeping knowledge to set up and may be more difficult for the novice to comprehend. However, once mastered, they are more flexible.

Available from most stationers are the **Cathedral, Guildhall** and **Cambridge Analysis** books, priced from about £10 to nearly £20 (depending on their size).

These books are suitable for both VAT and non-VAT registered businesses and come in different sizes (A4, A3.5 and A3), in different thicknesses (i.e. with more pages) and most importantly, with differing numbers of columns. Each page is identical. Choose a book with enough columns to suit your business – your accountant can advise you.

AT YEAR END
In addition to the routine book-keeping you have been doing throughout the year, at the "year end" there are important, but relatively simple, additional tasks to carry out. (The "year end" refers to the end of your financial (tax) year, rather than the calendar year).

For instance, if you hold any stock, raw material or part-completed work, you need to do a stock-take on the last day of your financial year. A "stock-take" involves counting all the different items you have and valuing them (normally at cost price). Another task is to list all your business creditors (people you owe money to) and debtors (people who owe you money) on that date.

Some of the better pre-printed accounts books have suitable pages and instructions to help you with these end of year tasks.

SOME BOOK-KEEPING TIPS . . .

- Start by entering your figures in pencil so you can correct errors easily. Ink them in later when you think it's right.

- Use only blue or black pen for your figures (this allows your accountant to use red and/or green).

- If you make a mistake with a figure (in ink) then you are supposed to draw a line through that figure and write the correct figure alongside. Don't use white-out fluid.

- If a figure in your accounts is negative (eg a bank balance in overdraft) then this is usually shown by brackets, eg (105.34) means –£105.34.

- If you are not VAT-registered, then throughout the accounts book you should record the full invoice values, inclusive of any VAT charged.

BOOK-KEEPING PROBLEMS

Here are several typical situations you might encounter when doing your own book-keeping:

(1) If you are a sole trader or partner and use your private car or home telephone partly for business use and wish to recover the business element of this expenditure, then you could pay the business portion of these bills by business cheque. At the end of your tax year you should be able to claim that proportion of the expenses, provided you have kept a record of business usage.

(2) If you pay for any business items using your personal credit card, when the card statement arrives, simply pay for those business items using a business cheque, and the remainder using a personal cheque.

(3) If you are unsure if an invoice is

The popular Best Small Business Accounts Book series and computer software.

regarded as a "business" expense, either ask your accountant or note it on the appropriate page of your accounts book.

(4) If you trade as a sole-trader or partnership and you want to transfer some surplus business money into a deposit account, then enter it in the accounts book under "Drawings". It should not affect your tax liability. The situation regarding a limited company is not so simple – ask your accountant.

(5) If you are using one of the blank heading, ruled accounts books, you may wonder what column headings to use. This question is best answered by your accountant as it depends on what type of business you are running, though there are many headings which are common to most businesses as can be seen in the headings chosen for

the BLUE BOOK illustrated on page 52.

And Finally . . . .

Do try very hard to keep your book-keeping up-to-date. If you find you are slipping behind, don't just give up! Stop what you are doing and try to fill in something very easy such as the current week's figures. Once you have broken the ice, go on to catch up with the past weeks you have missed.

*On the next three pages is a sample Month from the **Best Small Business Accounts Book** (the BLUE BOOK version). The pages are normally A4 (210 x 297mm) in size but have been reduced to fit here* ⇨

The Best Small Business Accounts Books

These are accounts books for non-VAT registered businesses. One book is for a *cash* business and its cover is colour-coded YELLOW. The other book is for a *credit* business and its cover is colour-coded BLUE.

The illustration (right) is a fictitious example given in the BLUE BOOK. Each month has 4 pages and these are shown (in reduced size) on this and the following two pages.

The BLUE BOOK is also available in a VAT VERSION (not shown here). The layout of the BLUE VAT BOOK is the same as the non-VAT version except there are additional columns for VAT, an extra 32 page VAT section and help to complete your VAT Returns.

Normally A4 (210 x 297mm) in size the page has been reduced to fit here.

Month 1   March 1996
month & year . . . .

© 1991 P. Hingston

SALES RECORD

Date of Invoice	Date Paid	Customer	Invoice Number	Invoice Total £	p
4		John Smith Ltd	026	82	75
5	4/5	B.I.G. Buyers & Co	027	962	43
8		Brown & Son	028	165	00
12		A. Supply Co	029	96	37
16	3/5	ABC Co	030	15	25
17		D. Jones	031	85	50
19		B.I.G. Buyers & Co	032	650	00
23		Brown & Son – CREDIT NOTE	033	(15	00)
23		D. Jones	034	23	15
~~26~~		~~A. Supply Co~~	~~035~~	~~90~~	~~00~~
26		A. Supply Co	036	95	00
31		ABC Co	037	160	26
31		John Smith Ltd	038	104	84
			Total	2425	55

(035 row marked: Cancelled)

SALES RECORD (continued)

Date of Invoice	Date Paid	Customer	Invoice Number	Invoice Total £	p

BANK RECORD

Bank Balance at start of Month			£	p
			1505	64

BANKINGS			Non-Sales		Sales	
Date	Details	Ref	£	p	£	p
4	Sales	136			220	48
8	From Building Soc'y a/c	137	1000	00		
11	Sales	138			382	50
19	Sales	139			955	25
26	Sales	140			986	60
31	Sales (Brown & Son) Invs 028/033				150	00
	Direct Credits ABC Co Inv 015				126	50
Totals			1000	00	2821	33
Total Bankings (ie Total Non-Sales + Sales Bankings)					3821	33

BANK DIRECT DEBITS etc			
Date	Details	Ref	
26	Bank Charges/Interest Quarterly Charge		65	00
1	HP/Lease/Loan repayments Car loan		145	00
Total			210	00

MONTH'S BANK BALANCE & STATEMENT CHECK			
Balance at start of Month + Total Bankings − Direct Debits		5116	97
Less Total Cheque Payments (total from overpage)		4491	52
Leaves: Balance at end of Month		625	45
BANK STATEMENT CHECK	Add total cheques not yet on Statement	400	00
	Less total bankings not yet on Statement	1136	60
	Leaves: Balance as per Statement	(111	15)

PETTY CASH

© 1991 P. Hingston

Money in Petty Cash at start of Month			£	p
			37	34

MONEY INTRODUCED DURING MONTH				
Date	Source of Money		Ref	
4	From Bank account	Chq	359	50	00
19	From Bank account	Chq	368	50	00
Total				100	00

PAYMENTS BY PETTY CASH		
Stock/Raw Materials		
Advertising/Promotion		
Cleaning		
Drawings/Salaries		
Electric/Gas/Heat		
Motor – Fuel £18 £15 £9 £12	54	00
– Other Expenses Repair	29	99
Postage/Parcels 98p £5 £6.50	12	48
Rent/Rates		
Repairs/Maintenance		
Staff Wages		
A. Helper	20	00
Stationery/Printing	6	75
Sundries		56
Telephone/Fax		
Travelling		
Any Other Expenses Trade magazine	2	00
Total Payments by Petty Cash	125	78

MONTH'S PETTY CASH BALANCE		
Petty Cash at start of Month + Money Introduced	137	34
Less Total Payments by Petty Cash	125	78
Less any surplus Cash paid into Bank		
Leaves: Money in Petty Cash at end of Month	11	56

Only a few entries are shown here to illustrate how these pages might be completed.

Please Turn Over ⇨

Date	Cheque Paid To	Chq No	TOTAL		Stock/ Raw Material		Advertising/ Promotion		Drawings/Sal/ NI/Pension		Electric/ Gas/Heat		All Motor Expenses		Postage/ Parcels			Rent/ Rates		Staff Wages & PAYE/NI		Stationery/ Printing		Sundries	
3	Auto Repair Co	357	70	05									70	05											
4	Self	358	100	00					100	00																
4	To Petty Cash	359	50	00																						
5	Paper Supplies Co	360	17	50																					17	50
8	ABC Co	361	128	26																			128	26		
9	The Phone Co	362	189	87																						
10	J. Smith (Supplies)	363	500	00	500	00																				
12	Petrol Station	364	139	99									139	99												
12	Parcel Services	365	158	27											158	27										
15	A. Brown	366	562	58			562	58																		
16	Computer Supplies Co	367	2125	00																						
19	To Petty Cash	368	50	00																						
25	Self	369	400	00					400	00																
	Total Cheque Payments for Month		4491	52	500	00	562	58	500	00			210	04	158	27							128	26	17	50

THIS chapter is to help you to cope with Income Tax and National Insurance contributions (including PAYE), Corporation Tax and VAT.

Note that these are not the only taxes that might confront you – for instance there is Capital Gains Tax and Business Rates which could apply. See the handy **Tax Data Page** at the end of this book and get professional advice from a qualified accountant.

 CAUTION Please note this chapter is for general guidance only and should not be regarded as a complete or authoritative statement on taxation. For more information, please consult an accountant, the Inland Revenue, Social Security or HM Customs & Excise.

WHO PAYS WHICH TAXES?

Depending upon the legal form of the business and whether or not there are employees, dictates which taxes are relevant and how these taxes are collected. So who pays what? . . . .

Sole Trader or Partnership (with no employees) In this case Income Tax is based on the business profits as declared in the annual Tax Return, and the Income Tax becomes due for payment in two instalments (currently in January and July).

In the case of a partnership, the profits of the business are divided equally between the partners, unless the Partnership Agreement says something to the contrary, and the liability for paying tax is the individual's.

In addition to Income Tax, a sole trader or partner is liable to pay Class 2 National Insurance contributions (which are a fixed weekly amount) and Class 4

contributions (which are profit related and calculated as a percentage of the profits in your Tax Return). Class 4 contributions are collected the same time as Income Tax. The Class 2 contributions are best paid by direct debit through your bank.

Sole Trader or Partnership (with employees) In addition to the above, if you have any employee who earns more than a certain amount then you must deduct National Insurance (and pay an Employers contribution). If they earn more than a certain (higher) amount then PAYE (Pay-As-You-Earn) also has to be operated so that any Income Tax due can be deducted.

Limited Company If you are a salaried Director you will almost always have to operate the PAYE system for yourself as well as any full-time staff you employ. The Income Tax and the National

Insurance contributions are paid through the PAYE system, *but note:* there are special rules for calculating Director's National Insurance contributions, in particular, Directors have an annual earnings period – refer to the DSS manual CA44(NI35) which should be included in your "New Employers Starter Pack".

In addition to these taxes a limited company is also liable to Corporation Tax which is a tax on profits, paid usually 9 months after the accounting period.

Cars and Fuel As an employer, if you provide a car or fuel for a Director or higher-paid employee's private use, you may be liable to pay Class 1A National Insurance contributions.

THE DIFFERENT TAXES

We now consider each of the main taxes in turn . . . .

INCOME TAX
(For Sole Traders or Partnerships)

Consider this example: assume your total annual sales (i.e. "turnover") is £50,000 but you had to spend £40,000 on stock, staff wages, advertising and other overheads, then you would have made a profit of £10,000. That would be declared in your Tax Return and the £10,000 is then regarded as the equivalent of a wage of £10,000. You are still entitled to your normal "personal allowances" and what is left is taxed at the prevailing rate of Income Tax.

Note that it makes no difference how much money you actually draw from the business – £25 per week or £250 per week, as your liability to Income Tax is solely dependent upon the *profitability* of your business!

The example we have discussed is shown graphically over the page.

Allowances In the above example we

Coping with Taxation

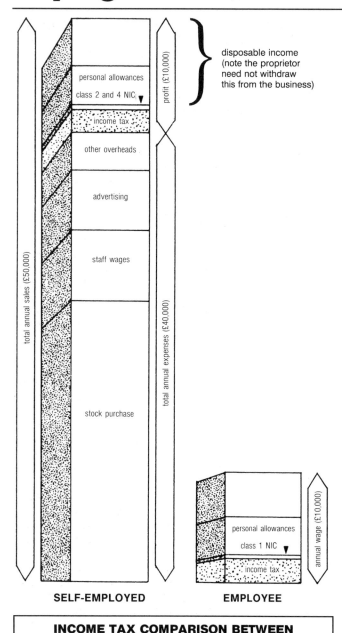

SELF-EMPLOYED

EMPLOYEE

disposable income
(note the proprietor
need not withdraw
this from the business)

personal allowances

class 2 and 4 NIC

income tax

other overheads

advertising

staff wages

stock purchase

total annual sales (£50,000)

profit (£10,000)

total annual expenses (£40,000)

personal allowances

class 1 NIC

income tax

annual wage (£10,000)

**INCOME TAX COMPARISON BETWEEN
SELF-EMPLOYED AND EMPLOYEE**

deducted £40,000 costs from the £50,000 annual sales figure to get a profit of £10,000 on which Income Tax is due. But what types of expenses and "overheads" can you deduct? For income tax purposes an important distinction is made between "revenue expenditure" and "capital expenditure".

Broadly speaking, "revenue expenditure" covers consumables and wages which would all normally be allowable deductions. This includes purchasing of stock or raw materials, staff wages, business rent and rates, phone bills, electricity and heating charges, advertising, stationery, insurance, professional fees, the replacement of worn-out tools by similar tools, necessary repairs and maintenance, interest on business loans and most vehicle expenses.

"Capital expenditure" covers once-off purchases of tangible assets such as business premises (including alterations), equipment, tools and vehicles. These are *not* automatically allowable – only certain categories are allowable, which are given a general writing-down capital allowance, which is currently 25%.

Only revenue expenditure which is *wholly and exclusively* for your business can be deducted from your annual sales figure when calculating your taxable profits. Items that are *not* allowable for income tax purposes include: your own drawings (i.e. your "wages"), food or other domestic expenditure, Income Tax, business entertainment etc.

Use of domestic phone or vehicle There are often situations with small businesses where expenditure is partly for business and partly for domestic purposes. Examples include the use of a car, the use of a telephone at your home and heat and lighting used in an "office" in your home. In the case of a car you could keep a vehicle log book in which you record every business trip (i.e. Date, Destination, Mileage and Purpose of Journey). With a phone you could also keep a simplified log of all business calls you make to back-up an itemised phone bill (if available). In this way you will have the proof to claim the correct proportion of the charges against tax. But before you start to log things, speak to your accountant as you may be giving yourself an unnecessary burden.

Construction Industry 714 Tax Certificate If you plan to work self-employed as a sub-contractor in the construction industry you may need to apply for this certificate. Without such a certificate the main contractor has to deduct tax at the basic rate from all payments and this may make obtaining sub-contract work difficult. Contact your local Inland Revenue office for more details.

Coping with Taxation

Coping With Income Tax Provided you keep accounts, as suggested in the previous chapter **Simple Book-keeping**, and you use an accountant to advise you, then you should be able to cope. The Inland Revenue's pamphlet IR28 is very readable and provides good advice for sole traders and partnerships. Remember to keep money aside to pay your tax! If your turnover is low, the Inland Revenue will accept simplified "three line accounts" (see the **Tax Data Page** at the end of this book).

NATIONAL INSURANCE
(For Sole Traders or Partnerships)
Even if you are already in employment and paying Class 1 National Insurance contributions, if you start a small business you may still need to pay a Class 2 contribution as well. However, if your self-employed earnings are less than what is called the "Small Earnings Exception", no Class 2 stamp need be paid. Refer to the **Tax Data Page** at the end of this book and if you are in this category, then contact your nearest Social Security office for more information.

Class 2 National Insurance contributions are paid separately to Class 1 so even if you employ someone, you will still have to pay your own Class 2 contributions separately (employees pay Class 1 contributions – see **PAYE** below). Visit your nearest Social Security office and ask for the appropriate leaflets for a self-employed person. You can elect to pay your Class 2 contributions monthly by direct debit from your bank account.

The Class 4 contribution which is based on the profitability of your business is generally assessed and collected by the Inland Revenue at the same time as your Income Tax. The Class 4 contribution is calculated as a percentage of the profits exceeding a certain figure but there is a maximum contribution limit.

PAYE
(For Limited Companies & all full-time Employees)
PAYE stands for Pay-As-You-Earn and is Income Tax and NI (National Insurance) deducted by an employer from the employee's wage packet. You will also have to pay an employer's NI contribution. If you employ staff or are a limited company contact your nearest PAYE office (look under "Inland Revenue" in the Phone Book), and ask them for a "New Employers Starter Pack" which contains full instructions and forms.

Paying PAYE/NI When you register for PAYE you will usually be sent a Payslip Booklet with instructions as to how to pay the tax. The amount due should cover both Income Tax and National Insurance, including the employers contribution. Most employers have to pay this monthly but if your monthly payments are below a certain threshold (see the **Tax Data Page** at the back of this book) you can elect to pay quarterly. For further advice, contact your PAYE office.

CORPORATION TAX
(For Limited Companies only)
This is a tax on the profits of a business in much the same way as Income Tax is calculated for a sole trader or partnership. Corporation Tax is normally paid 9 months after the end of the accounting year.

If as a Director you take a wage out of the company, the wage will be liable to Income Tax which will have to be deducted from your wage packet under the PAYE scheme mentioned above. Shareholders in the company can be paid "dividends" out of the profits of the company but the tax rules are complex with ACT (Advance Corporation Tax) having to be paid by the company – this requires your accountant's advice.

VALUE ADDED TAX (VAT)
First refer to the item on VAT at the end of the **Making it Legal** chapter. The VAT "bible" is the VAT Guide (Notice 700) which will tell you all you need to know about VAT. Remember that you do not need to register for VAT unless your taxable turnover exceeds (or is likely to exceed) a certain figure – see the **Tax Data Page**. Registration is also required if at any time it appears you will exceed the threshold in the next 30 days. If you need to register for VAT then you must keep additional records to those you would otherwise keep for the business. In particular you need to record all taxable goods and services that you buy and sell as part of the business. There is no set way to do this but they must be such that you can fill in your VAT Return and so the VAT man can understand them. Ask your accountant about this or your local VAT office. In addition, as a VAT-registered trader you will have to give proper tax invoices unless you sell direct to the public in which case you only need to provide a tax invoice if requested. The VAT leaflet "Keeping Records and Accounts" gives more information and is very readable.

Coping with Taxation

Note that as a VAT-registered trader you can normally only reclaim "input tax" if you have a proper tax invoice.

If you are registered for VAT then you must normally make a return to the Customs & Excise each quarter on a Form VAT 100 (usually referred to as the "VAT Return"). You have one month from the end of the quarterly period to complete and return the form and to make your payment (if you owe VAT). If your "input tax" exceeds your "output tax" total, then once you have submitted your VAT Return you can expect a payment from HM Customs & Excise. Finally, do remember that there are stiff penalties for late submission of VAT Returns.

Tax Point   An important aspect to remember when completing the VAT Return is the "Tax Point" (i.e. the date or "time of supply") of a transaction. In practice this is normally the date given on the invoice (provided the invoice is issued promptly) but note that legally this is only one of the possible relevant dates, i.e. when goods were supplied or a service completed are other possible Tax Points. Provided a Tax Point is within the quarter on which you are reporting then it has to be included in your VAT Return (even if no payment has yet been made!) unless you are using the "Cash Accounting Scheme".

Tax Invoices   In general a VAT invoice (usually called a "tax invoice") should have a unique identifying number and give the supplier's name, address and VAT number, the date the invoice is issued, the type of supply (eg sale or rental), the tax point, a full description and quantity of the goods or services, the rate of cash discount offered (if any), the rate of VAT, the total (excluding VAT), the amount of VAT and the total payable. The invoice should also give the customer's name and address unless you mainly sell direct to the public and the invoice total is under £100.

If selling to other EC countries, the customer's VAT number and country code must appear on your invoice (in addition to your own VAT number with a GB prefix).

The "Cash Accounting Scheme"   This special scheme allows a small business to account for VAT on the basis of payments received and made rather than tax invoices issued and received. This can be a particular help if you give your customers long periods of credit.

The "Annual Accounting Scheme"   Small businesses with a taxable turnover less than a certain threshold may be eligible to opt for this scheme whereby the business can account for its VAT by making regular interim payments then completing one annual VAT Return with a final payment, adjusted to balance the account.

KEY POINT

For more information on these schemes and VAT in general, it is essential you contact your local HM Customs & Excise ■

HOME-BASED BUSINESS IDEAS

Chapters

T HIS section of the book is devoted to business ideas for you to consider. These ideas are intended to not only provide a source of usable ideas, but also whet the appetite, illustrate just what can be done and possibly act as a catalyst to trigger your own imagination.

If you have the time to count all the business ideas listed in this section you will discover there are more than a hundred, plus many adaptations. If you stop to think for a moment, you will probably realise that you yourself know quite a few people who carry on businesses, large or small, from their homes.

What are these people doing? There are, of course, thousands of ways of making an honest pound or two from a home-based business. In fact the sheer ingenuity of people in dreaming up new ways to make money is quite amazing.

Some of the business ideas in this book require specific skills or training, but that is unavoidable. Other ideas can be taken up by virtually anyone who is willing to make the effort to learn the basics.

We have tried to select a range of business ideas to cater for both men and women, of different ages, with different skills, in different financial situations and living in different types of housing in different parts of the country. We hope therefore that you will find something that interests you.

What business should you do?
When you are considering self-employment, don't just think of doing what you have done in the past as an employee.

Instead, ask yourself what there is a demand for and that you could do (and enjoy doing it, as well)?

FURTHER READING Space limits the information given for each business idea, but Kogan Page publishes books on many specific businesses and their books are available through any bookshop.

Hobbies If you develop your hobby into a business, it could mushroom and before you know where you are you have a major business on your hands. At that stage you may decide that you prefer to keep it as a hobby, albeit a paying one, and not to expand it any further.

The thing about turning a hobby into a business is that it can spoil the hobby for you. There are few people who change their hobby into a business without later having some regrets.

THE BUSINESS IDEAS CHAPTERS
Chapter: A-Z The ideas in this first chapter have been arranged alphabetically. It is relevant to note that the ideas were not simply dreamed up for the benefit of this book. We know, or have known, people doing these businesses, some full-time, some part-time. We consulted many of them when writing this book.

Chapter: Arts & Crafts This is an important area of home-based businesses as the majority of the 25,000 or so

Business Ideas – Introduction

craftworkers in Britain are home-based, and this number excludes the thousands of artists. The industry includes many part-time as well as full-time people.

Chapter: Direct Selling   This includes selling by party-plan, networking, door-to-door and personal referral. Most people involved in direct selling are self-employed and home-based. It is estimated that maybe as many as half a million people do direct selling, mainly on a part-time basis.

Chapter: Franchising   Although franchising, as an industry is large, only a small proportion are home-based, however it still represents an interesting option for people who want to become self-employed.

Chapter: Teaching   There are so many things that can be taught from home, and teaching can also provide additional income to another home-based business.

Chapter: Writing   Many people would like to write for a living, but to be published is not easy and this chapter provides some useful advice for budding authors.

Exclusions
The business ideas in this book exclude teleworking (where you are usually an employee of a company, but work from home). Also excluded are the professions (such as vets, dentists, accountants, surveyors and osteopaths), some of whom practice from their homes.

Another group that are excluded are trades (such as plumbers and electricians) as they too need special training and qualifications, but we have included "Handyman" and "Painting & Decorating" as business ideas as those can be done by a keen DIY enthusiast, who is prepared to learn.

We have also excluded many businesses which will be obvious to the people who could do them (for instance, babysitters, entertainers, models, music teachers, tele-sales people). And finally we exclude company "reps" who, although they may be home-based, are usually employees ∎

ACCOUNTS BOOK-KEEPING

There are many small and medium-sized businesses that cannot afford to employ their own accountants and book-keepers. They use an accountant to prepare their tax return each year, but during the year they need someone with book-keeping skills to maintain their accounts.

There was a time when this type of work could be done by anyone of reasonable intelligence with a pencil and notebook. However, these days book-keeping is much more complex because of the requirements of the Inland Revenue (and H.M. Customs & Excise if registered for VAT).

Although formal qualifications are not required the reality is that, unless you have either substantial experience or some training, your work will not be satisfactory to your clients. Most people who operate in this field are either working towards accountancy qualifications or they have worked as book-keepers before retiring from the workforce.

If you want to consider training to become a qualified accountant, you could contact The Chartered Association of Certified Accountants, who provide a structured training programme.

The type of business clients who require book-keeping services will usually have quite complex accounting systems or computerised accounts.

Any size of business may use outside help to do their VAT Returns and a number of quite large businesses use a book-keeping service to prepare their payroll details.

You could also prepare tax returns but only qualified accountants can do the audits required by limited companies.

Capital requirements are fairly low but at a minimum you would need office equipment including a printing calculator, a filing cabinet, a telephone with an answering machine; a reasonably powerful PC computer with a good general accounting package and a spreadsheet package, and a private place in your home that is not accessible to others as the information you are dealing with is confidential.

The key factor with this business is reliability. The people using your service will expect the work to be done promptly and conscientiously. You have a legal responsibility to your clients so you must ensure that your work is accurate. If your client suffers damage as a result of your failure to do the work properly, you could be sued, so professional indemnity insurance is strongly advisable. Also, don't pretend you know more than you do, as that can be dangerous for all concerned.

To get clients, word-of-mouth publicity is the best form of advertising, as is often the case, but this takes time. A listing in the Yellow Pages is another way to let people know about your service. General newspaper advertising in the local papers will probably be a waste of money.

ADDRESS

The address of The Chartered Association of Certified Accountants is given at the end of this book.

BEAUTICIAN

If you plan to see clients in your own home, this will usually raise problems as your local authority may regard it as a salon and will then require you to comply with a whole range of regulations. The alternative is to visit clients in their own homes.

Two good things about this business are first, it is sociable and it makes one feel good to help people and second, it is a cash business, so no bad debts. A possible downside is the long hours and evening work. Also some customers can be very difficult to please.

An essential requirement is indemnity insurance in case a client is injured and tries to sue you. The cost of the insurance premium depends on what therapies you plan to provide, for instance electrolysis is generally regarded (by the insurers) as more risky. Most insurers will insist on seeing your certificates before they will insure you, so you do need to be properly trained and have an appropriate qualification.

To work out your charges, find out what local salons are charging and then charge a little less. People will certainly not expect to pay more than going to a salon, even if they are having the convenience of the treatment in their own homes.

Word of mouth is the best way to get new customers, so hand a leaflet to everyone you know and all your clients. If you know a freelance hairdresser who is visiting clients in their homes, perhaps you can each give out the other person's leaflets. Newspaper advertising tends to be a waste of money.

ADDRESS

The International Health & Beauty Council (whose address is at the end of this book) have a leaflet on training to become a Beauty Therapist.

BED & BREAKFAST

If you have spare bedroom accommodation in your house and you are located in the right area, then B&B can provide useful additional income. However, your B&B sign will attract little custom unless you are located in either a tourist area or where business people frequent, and ideally both.

Your B&B clientele can be: "passing trade" (that is people who see your sign, need a room for the night and stop), customers referred through your local Tourist Information Office and "repeat" customers. Your local Tourist Information Office (if you have one) can probably give you an idea as to likely demand, what people are prepared to pay

and what facilities they look for. Remember that tourism is seasonal in most parts of the country.

Speak to your local Fire Prevention Officer to find out what Fire Regulations might apply, if any. Contact your Environmental Health Officer about the Food Hygiene Regulations. Consider attending the one-day Food Hygiene training course run by most colleges. And check with the Planning Department as permission may be required and there is usually control on signs. If you have a mortgage, discuss your idea with the mortgage lender. Check your title deeds to ensure there is no restriction preventing you from doing B&B.

It is also important to check the insurance aspects with a registered insurance broker. In particular you want to be insured in case a guest gets hurt accidentally while on your premises. The ability to be nice to people, cook a good breakfast and be happy changing beds and cleaning are the main skills you need, though the work can seem at times like a repetitive slog. Guests rightly expect the accommodation to be meticulously clean. You need to consider if you will permit smoking in your bedrooms.

Assuming no Fire Certificate is required and no alterations, then no major capital outlay is required other than making sure the bedroom decor is fresh, buying new bed linen, ensuring there is tea and coffee making facilities in each room and possibly installing TVs. Ideally you should have a separate bathroom for guests. If your spare bedrooms are large enough you may be able to create small en-suite bathrooms (actually they tend to have showers rather than baths to save space and hot water). This work will usually require a Building Warrant.

Customers may not always be as careful as you are with your belongings so anticipate the cost of damage to furnishings etc. Having strangers around your home can disrupt your domestic life and there are security implications too. If you have beautiful and expensive ornaments, they might "walk out" with your guests. It might be an idea to take a note of car registration numbers as a precaution.

As it takes time to build up repeat business and attract new customers by word-of-mouth, for the first few years doing B&B usually only gives a secondary income but after that it could support you. If you intend to do B&B professionally then consider taking a course at a local college.

One upside of this business is you can make new friends who return year after year, and even send you Xmas cards.

BURGLAR ALARM INSTALLING

The level of crime these days is such that many people are concerned that their homes or workplaces are going to be broken into, so there is a considerable market for burglar alarm installation work (and related activities).

However there are several catches. First, and probably most importantly, many alarms are installed due to pressure from insurers and they usually insist that the company doing the installation is a member of a trade association. The second problem with this service is that people seek peace of mind so will often opt for a known, established alarm company.

The next problem is that this is very much a "negative" purchase as people don't like making the decision to install an alarm and they certainly don't like spending much money on it. Finally, there is a great deal of competition (just take a quick look in the Yellow Pages under "Burglar Alarms").

Therefore the actual market you can tap into is much reduced so you need to research your local market carefully. You may be able to compete on price due to your low overheads, your ability to sell, the quality of your installation and how you treat your customers.

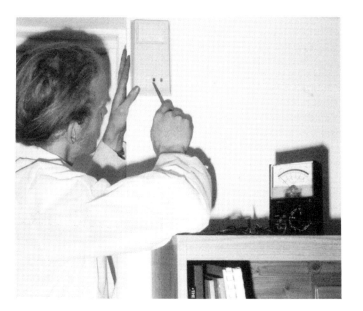

To get into this business you need to know what you are doing, to have the appropriate expertise. A basic understanding of electronics is essential, as is some DIY ability. There are many books on the subject and visits to major trade shows, such as IFSEC, is essential.

Additional business can be obtained by fitting mechanical security devices such as window locks, and by installing smoke detectors. If possible, try to get customers on to an annual maintenance scheme to give you some ongoing income, but a drawback is they will call you out at all hours due to inevitable false alarms. Thankfully today's technology has reduced the incidence of false alarms dramatically.

ADDRESS The IFSEC organiser's phone number and the address of SITO (Security Industry Training Organisation), are given at the end of this book.

BUSINESS CONSULTANT

Since the 1980's many executives in British industry have been made redundant or have taken early retirement. At the same time, the management needs of many companies have increased due to company reorganisations, buy-outs, new EC legislation and the continuing rapid changes in the market-place. Thus these companies have been users of business consultants. Government agencies have also been great providers of work for consultants.

Small businesses are often short of good management expertise and so there have been several government initiatives to subsidise consultancy assistance for such companies. This has benefited both small businesses and consultants. Find out if any subsidy exists as that would help you to sell your services to appropriate firms.

Although there may appear to be lots of potential work for consultants, things can be tough for someone setting out on this venture. Small to medium sized firms often don't perceive they need outside management advice and if they do they usually cannot afford it (unless it's subsidised). Meanwhile larger firms tend to call in the big consultancy groups rather than newly started home-based consultants. Finally, there are an awful lot of consultants out there! So success to begin with

Business Ideas – A-Z

depends very much on your existing contacts and many consultants in fact start with work provided by their old employers. One way to succeed may be to specialise in some area rather than being just a general "management" or "business" consultant.

Remember to speak to an insurance broker about the need for professional indemnity insurance.

ADDRESS

The address of the Institute of Management Consultants is given at the end of this book.

BUYING AN EXISTING BUSINESS

This is another way for people to get into business for the first time and it can be successful, as it short-cuts much of the difficult start-up process. You learn of businesses for sale from adverts in local newspapers, through your local business development agency and by word of mouth. See also the publication *Daltons Weekly* for village shops, guest houses and other businesses which are combined with homes.

As with anything in business, caution is necessary. Ask yourself why a business is being sold if it is any good? If the business is doing even reasonably well it is more likely to be taken over by a close friend or a member of the proprietor's family. That is not to say that good or potentially good businesses do not come onto the market but you need to know fully about what you are taking on and why it is being sold. If you don't know much about the particular trade or business you are considering, you are very vulnerable.

One great advantage of buying over an existing business is that the need for doing a full market research is diminished (but not eliminated) because you have access to real trading figures gleaned from the accounts of the business. However, trading conditions vary constantly and you must do some market research to ensure that market conditions are not likely to vary adversely for the foreseeable future.

What will the business cost to buy? In very general terms a business has a value equal to its Stock (valued at cost, not retail price) plus Machinery & Equipment (valued at its depreciated price) plus Goodwill. This last one is the really

The value of a business should not be shrouded in mystery!

grey area of valuation. Goodwill equals the value of the business less the tangible business assets. It is a measure of the momentum of profitability that the business has built up. It should therefore be based on the proven profits of the business, looking at the last few years (since the business may be growing rapidly or declining). If a typical net profit (before tax) figure can be agreed, then the goodwill can be valued for a small business at usually between 1 and 5 times the profit figure. The actual multiplier chosen is dependent upon all the other factors involved in the sale, such as the perceived growth potential of the business, any patents or designs owned by the business, and the size of the existing customer base. Goodwill is very negotiable and if it relates closely to the former owner that part will be lost when he or she leaves in which case it would be worth less.

Remember to get advice from an accountant, who should go through the last few years accounts of the business and explain to you all the salient features. Be sure you also understand any tax implications of the purchase and you may also need to read a copy of the VAT leaflet "Transfer of a Business as a Going Concern". If there are any existing staff, get professional advice before you go any further.

It's vital you always get good legal advice when buying a business as there are potential pitfalls – especially if you are being asked to purchase a limited company where you will be acquiring its liabilities in addition to its assets.

CATERING

Assuming that you have the expertise and can afford to invest the necessary capital to set up this type of business, catering can be a good home-based money earner though it will take time to become established.

You may be catering for special occasions, such as weddings, or providing lunches for local business boardroom meetings or other commercial events. You might have to cope with feeding just a handful of people or several hundred.

Many catering businesses are now quite complex. In some cases the caterer has become a party planner, arranging everything from intimate breakfasts at home on couples' wedding anniversaries to corporate luncheons for 400 business people. As a caterer you may simply prepare one of the courses, buying in the rest of the food, or you may cook several courses and supply a marquee, all furniture, glassware and dishes. Regardless of the detail of your business, there are two key factors. You must comply with all the health and food regulations and you must know your market.

There are stringent regulations regarding most aspects of handling, preparing and selling food. For instance, equipment, premises, food handlers, storage, working methods, labelling etc are all covered. It is essential you talk to your local Environmental Health Officer at the very beginning of your project and long before you start your business.

Your kitchen will need to meet certain standards and no pets are allowed. It's wise to keep food purchased for the business completely separate from food to be consumed by you and your family. If not, any food found in the kitchen will be deemed as for consumption by the public. This could land you in the proverbial soup if one of your family left a mouldy sandwich in the fridge and it's found by an inspector.

If you use the client's kitchen then although it is up to them

10 TIPS TO SAVE ON CATERING COSTS

1. **People eat more at buffet-style meals than at sit-down meals. They fill plates quickly as they pass along. So put the expensive foods at the far end of the table.**

2. **Moulds and mousses make expensive foods like lobster and crabmeat go further.**

3. **Provide fruit punch, as it is relatively cheap to make and reduces consumption of more expensive drinks.**

4. **Edible centre-pieces such as food trees cut down the expense of decorations.**

5. **Be careful in quoting a price, particularly where seasonal foods are involved. Make the quotation – in writing – on a "per head" basis and count the number of people present at the event. If it is more than expected, point this out politely to the client on the spot. Do not leave the matter until the moment of payment.**

6. **Request a deposit when the booking is made and make it clear that, as in a restaurant, payment of the balance must be made at the end of the occasion. The usual deposit is half of the total cost. Since one large bad cheque can just about put you out of business you may even ask for full payment seven days in advance. However, this may affect your sales unless you have a really strong reputation for reliability.**

7. **Offer a refund if the occasion is cancelled. This may be a full refund if seven days' notice is given, a partial refund up to three days before the event. Have the refund conditions printed on your quotation sheet.**

8. **List the hours you will be in attendance, the time you will serve the meal and mention your charge for any overtime.**

9. **Include in your written quotation the name of the person to whom you are responsible. You cannot take orders from a committee of people or a whole family. Naming one person in authority (and getting their signature on the agreement) could help you if you have a dispute.**

10. **Keep a notebook containing details of each party. Include problems that occurred and any extra costs that arose unexpectedly.**

to ensure the kitchen complies with the regulations, as caterer you are responsible for your own practices and so the onus is on you to ensure that there are no deficiences in the kitchen that could affect you.

You need to realise that commercial cooking is not the same as domestic cooking as there is risk and the legal implications are onerous. Discuss liability insurance with a registered insurance broker.

Various colleges run one-day Food Hygiene training courses. You really should attend one and do so before you start your business.

If you are asked to provide alcohol, it is essential you get advice from your local authority as to the need for a licence.

The catering business is often a slow starter because business is usually built upon word of mouth publicity and many clients are once-only for 21st birthdays or weddings. Some ideas that have been suggested for building your catering business are as follows.

Advertise in the Yellow Pages and send circulars to local clubs and organisations. Your local council usually has a list of the name and address of the secretary of each club or community group in your area. If you are targeting business functions, you will need to write and approach appropriate companies in your area.

The quality of the food is critically important. People will remember the food long after the event. If something is not right it will be talked about and will do your business a great deal of harm. Buy only the best quality ingredients and do not try to cut corners. In the final analysis the ingredients are not a major part of your costs. People expect professional caterers to provide food which looks lavishly expensive. They will be disappointed if it only looks like the food they can prepare at home. Presentation is as important as flavour.

Sales support material is a great help with coloured photographs in a portfolio showing some of your past successes. You might even get some of the really good photos enlarged (as that looks more impressive). Always remember that in any business it is far better to under-promise then over-perform, than to over-promise and under-perform. The former gives you a great reputation, the latter will lead to disappointed clients and bad publicity.

Sample menus which show that you are up with the trends also help. These may include health lunches. Few people may order them but the fact that you have indicated an awareness of health issues will impress the clients. Some caterers extend into specialist areas such as Kosher meals and Chinese dishes. Remember that the law requires that the food you provide is exactly what you say it is.

As in any business cost control is very important. Some tips that have come from people already doing well in the catering field are given in the box on the previous page.

CHILD MINDING

Unlike baby sitting, this is where children will be left by a parent at your home. Not surprisingly, this type of activity is subject to a number of stringent controls. In practice this means the local authorities may require you to spend a considerable amount of money adapting your home and buying essential equipment prior to starting.

The requirements and regulations relating to premises and facilities are strict and you should make early enquiries with the Social Work department of your local authority. But be warned, this may put you off the idea completely. The Social Work department will alert the Police, Fire Safety Officer and Environmental Health Officer who may all wish to visit you.

The authorities are very fussy about the size of house and garden, bathroom facilities, where the children are to eat and play, the existence of pets etc. You will need to meet a number of stringent fire safety regulations too. The bill for all this work could be as high as £5-10,000 in some cases.

One good feature of this business is that demand far exceeds supply in most parts of the country so you should have little difficulty filling your places. However, the number of children you can look after will be restricted and even what you charge is controlled so it all tends to limit what you can earn from child minding.

If you are interested, first you must be acceptable to the local authority as a fit person to care for children and be registered as a child minder. Of course, it helps if you have had considerable experience with children and you like them. Other people's children never seem as good as your own, so if your own were a burden, this is probably not the business for you.

In this business, insurance cover is essential and can be

arranged through the National Child Minding Association.

Once you are operating you will find the key factors for success are safety of the children and their happiness in being with you. A parent often feels a bit guilty about leaving their child with a child minder and it will be the last straw if the child has to be dragged kicking and screaming out of the car each morning.

One major problem with child minding is the way in which it ties you to the house and keeps you on the run for most of the day. Poor payment by parents can be another snag.

ADDRESS

The address of the National Child Minding Association is given at the end of this book.

CITY SIGHTSEEING

If you live in or near a city or town that is a tourist attraction, then this business idea may interest you. There are numerous possibilities for tours in most cities. There are historic buildings, gift shops, the botanical gardens, fashion shops, unique

Edinburgh: a popular tourist destination.

restaurants for lunch, museums and unusual or typical local manufacturing companies that may welcome visitors.

This service will appeal to many organisations, senior citizens, visitors, overseas students and other tourists. If the groups are small you could hire a minibus. You will need business cards, brochures and insurance (the last item in case one of your clients hurts themselves whilst on a tour).

It is possible to do this on a walking tour basis if you do not want to use a vehicle, particularly in city centres where parking is difficult anyway. You could meet them at a particular point, probably a hotel or tourist office, then conduct them on a walking tour to see some of the highlights of the city. Some retailers and restaurants that you select may be prepared to give you commission for bringing trade to them, but you should not compromise the quality of your tour.

To be successful, you need to tie into organisations that are already handling visitors to the city. So you may do a deal with some of the major hotels or tourist information offices that they promote your tours (for a commission). They might even take bookings for you.

CLASSIC CAR RESTORATION

Unlike modern cars that depreciate at an alarming rate, many classic cars maintain their value and some appreciate in price. Besides being investments they can also give their owners great pleasure. The late 1980's saw the value of many classic cars rise far beyond their realistic value due to speculators entering the market, but that bubble has passed and prices are now more stable.

Not all enthusiasts have the time or necessary skill to restore an old car so there are two business opportunities. You could either buy a suitable car that is in poor condition, restore it then sell it or you could restore cars that belong to others. It may pay to specialise in one marque so that you eventually get a reputation as an expert on those cars.

To consider this business idea, you would need to have car restoration skills or be prepared to learn them. There is insufficient margin to allow you to subcontract all the work so other than specialist jobs, such as trimming and spraying, expect to do most of it yourself. You will also need to know

An Austin-Healey 3000 undergoing restoration.

the market for classic cars, in particular which cars are worth restoring and where to acquire them at a sensible price.

You will obviously need to have a garage or the use of one, the appropriate tools and the capital to buy your first vehicle (unless you are going to restore someone else's car). Unless you have another source of income you will also need cash to survive on while you carry out the restoration. If you plan to buy a car then restore it for resale, the time this will take could be considerable. You would need to budget carefully to meet your domestic bills during the many months that will elapse between you first starting to look for a suitable car, restoring it and finally finding a buyer.

If you are only doing one car at a time and adopt a low profile working in your garage, this should not upset the neighbours provided you don't make a noise or create other problems. The use of heat (as in welding) or dangerous chemicals are best avoided. If working in your garage, it may be prudent to ensure that your insurers and mortgage lender (or landlord) know and approve what you are doing.

CLEANING

One of the major attractions of a cleaning business is that it requires only a small amount of capital to get started. This,

however, means that there are a lot of other firms competing for business and profit margins can be tight.

You could restrict your activities to houses and flats, or you could do cleaning of shops or offices. One factor that may influence your choice is that domestic cleaning is done mainly in the day time and commercial premises are cleaned mainly at night.

No special skills are required, just hard conscientious work, though certain cleaning techniques can reduce the workload. These are learned by experience or through training courses run by cleaning equipment manufacturers.

One lady who runs her own small business that cleans homes offers the following 12 hints:

1. Leaflets put through letterboxes are more effective than newspaper adverts. She herself uses a card-size coloured leaflet with a cartoon and just the bare details of her service. She recommends you don't mention prices or put too much on the leaflet as people will not bother to read it.

2. Charge less for regular clients because weekly services are easier to maintain than irregular clients.

3. Set out clearly in writing the services that will be performed and then try to do a little more than that.

4. Try to get the people out of the house while you clean. If they are in the house it makes the work much slower.

5. Be aware that many people are nervous about having strangers in their home. Show references from satisfied clients to help allay such fears.

6. Wear a uniform with your business name on it and a name badge.

7. If you get a complaint, don't argue with the client. Apologise and offer to refund the charge with a free repeat service. Customer satisfaction is absolutely critical.

8. Cleaning flats is the most profitable work and the whole job can often be done in a couple of hours.

9. Have your own equipment, then there are no problems with faulty appliances, shortages of materials, etc.

10. Do tasks in a certain order with a checklist. This is more efficient and will prevent tasks being overlooked.

11. If the place is really filthy, don't worry if you cannot make it absolutely spotless. People who live in those conditions will probably be pleased just to have it improved.

12. Don't attempt to clean the outsides of windows above the ground floor (too risky) or to shampoo valuable carpets (risky unless you have the necessary specialist knowledge).

If you want to do commercial cleaning, send letters to businesses in your area and then follow this up by phone to try to arrange a meeting.

A specialised area is cleaning homes when people move. This is very straightforward work because the house will be empty. Contact can be made with these people by leaving cards with estate agents and advertising on the property pages. The average empty house can be cleaned in about half a day.

To work out your pricing, find out what the competition is charging and fix yours accordingly. Note that many commercial contracts are let by competitive tender so there is a danger that you may quote too low and be locked into an unprofitable contract. One matter for concern is that the cleaning business can be very competitive and price cutting by competitors can undermine your profits and client base.

You should be familiar with the COSHH regulations (which control substances hazardous to health). Note that if you plan to clean food premises, then the Food Hygiene Regulations apply (speak to an Environmental Health Officer). As you are working in other people's premises, good liability insurance is worth considering.

COMPUTER EXPERT

This book is being written using a computer. What would I do if the computer suddenly failed or behaved erratically? After some moments of panic I would attempt to solve the problem myself but if I was unable to get the machine to work properly then I would need to call a computer expert to repair it. Some computer users would also need help when choosing new software. The computer expert should be able to advise which package to buy and could set it up on the customer's computer as such a task can itself be quite daunting to the uninitiated user. A computer expert can also advise on the purchase of new computer equipment.

So there are several ways in which a computer buff can generate income. The main problem is getting the initial business. In time your reputation will spread by word of mouth and existing customers will return for new software and to upgrade their hardware, but getting the first customers will take some time and effort. If you were in this business, you could also try giving computing tuition privately or at the local college, which would be a good way to make new business contacts.

To be a computer expert or "consultant" you need an excellent knowledge of computers, their operating systems and software packages. You also need to have a great deal of experience in solving computer problems. This is not the business to be in if you only *think* you know what you are doing. Formal qualifications are of little significance.

Minimal capital is required to start. Your knowledge is your capital, though you probably need a good PC computer.

Note that only about one third of small businesses in the UK currently use computers. Finally, if this business idea appeals to you, it may be wise to consider taking out liability insurance to protect yourself.

Business Ideas – A-Z

CONSERVATORY & FITTED KITCHEN CONSULTANT

Adding a conservatory to your house or redoing the kitchen are both high on the priorities for many homeowners. The snag being that the work is expensive and the choice of suppliers bewildering. Furthermore we have all read too many stories of people being ripped off by cowboys.

This is where an independent and knowledgeable consultant can provide a useful service that most customers will appreciate. The consultant sees the job through from the initial sales lead to the completed job. Usually the consultant gets quotations from different builders or kitchen fitters, discusses these with the client, places the order, supervises the job then bills the client at the end.

If interested in this business you need to be knowledgeable and you probably have a background in joinery or building work. Not much capital is required as the client pays you on completion of the job and the conservatory builder or kitchen fitter normally gives you credit terms (though they may not do so to begin with).

As is so often the case in business, most work comes by recommendation from previous satisfied clients. Advertising and special promotions can generate additional sales leads.

A major downside is the cut-throat nature of this business with a lot of under-cutting in prices by competitors.

COURIER SERVICE

The courier service is a very competitive business and prices reflect that (i.e. there is not much profit), but there is a demand for this business and you may be able to find a niche. For instance, most courier firms do not provide a week-end or night service which may be useful to some customers.

In cities and the larger towns you will frequently see couriers on motor-cycles, making deliveries and running messages for businesses. Some of these services are very specialised. For example, there are couriers who only handle legal documents, transferring them from one firm of solicitors to another. Some couriers are involved mainly in the home delivery of pizzas. Advertising agencies and graphics studios are other people who use couriers, in this case to move artwork on tight deadlines.

Many courier firms are not as specialised, taking on more general work where people just ring up when they require the service. For the small operator, who is just starting out in the business, those smaller, less regular jobs that do not interest the larger courier firms may be one way into the business. Some couriers augment their work by sub-contracting for larger, national companies, doing their local pick-ups and deliveries.

If you are a motor-cyclist you could do this business on your own with the aid of a mobile phone. Alternatively you could simply manage the business and employ riders (with their own motor-cycles) to collect and deliver. Either way you need to organise the work so the minimum time is spent on each job.

The key factors are reliability, low price and speed. You must be able to deliver in a short period of time, with little warning. People mainly use courier services because the normal postal service is too slow for them.

To get some idea of the scale of charges, it might be worth calling one or more couriers and getting each to do a small job for you. Observe the way in which they operate and the paperwork that they use.

To get started you could call on businesses in your area, explaining your service. You might consider a listing in the Yellow Pages and getting some business cards and price lists printed. You will also need some triplicate consignment books so that when you pick up an item you can give the sender a signed receipt, issue a copy to the person receiving the item and keep the third copy (with the recipient's signature) so you can raise the appropriate invoice.

A catchy business name and perhaps a uniform will help you look professional.

DISC JOCKEY

One of the great things about being a disc jockey is that you get to attend parties all the time. However the cost of setting up is substantially greater than many other home-based businesses and you will probably need a van or estate car to carry your equipment around.

The way to obtain business at first is to send leaflets to schools and other organisations, such as clubs and colleges. You could also try advertising in the local newspapers. To get into the wedding reception market you need to build up a good relationship with local photographers, caterers, bridal salons and hotels where wedding receptions are held. Always have business cards available to hand out.

When someone wants to use your service, you should have them sign a contract. Get proper legal advice as to the wording of this document. The contract should describe the function, the location, the time you can enter the premises to set up your kit, the times that your performance should start and end, when you can dismantle your equipment and the deposit you require. It is wise never to accept a job without a deposit. Also be wary of teenagers who make bookings for their homes or schools without adult permission.

One DJ who has operated his business from his home for the last three years offers some tips for success:

1. Do your own work. If people book you to do the function, don't send a substitute along. It's you they want, so do it yourself!

2. Dress and act professionally. If it's a formal occasion, dress accordingly.

3. Don't drink on the job.

4. Develop good PR skills. Often you are serving as the master of ceremonies so you need to know who's who and personalise your programme as much as possible.

5. Before the event discuss with the client what music they want, any special requests they have and the itinerary of the event. Make sure that the music is planned for their interest, not yours.

6. Be selective about your music for young people. Don't play music that someone is going to find offensive, especially songs that are drug related.

7. The event you are playing at may be a very special occasion for someone – so be sensitive.

8. Really try hard. Good service is the key to success. Be someone your clients can count on. Make sure that you are on time, follow your client's instructions and be tidy. If someone complains the music is too loud, then turn it down.

Remember that normal car insurance will not cover you should your vehicle be broken into and your valuable disco equipment be stolen or damaged, so you need to discuss this aspect with you insurers.

As a DJ you may need a licence and pay royalties – contact the two organisations below.

ADDRESS

The addresses of The Performing Right Society and Phonographic Performance Ltd are given at the end of this book.

DOG GROOMING

There are quite a number of dog-owners who have valuable dogs but find it impossible to keep up with the grooming – hence this business opportunity.

To start, no formal qualifications are required, but there are some courses advertised (normally aimed at the pet owners themselves). If you are simply going to run a dog grooming service from your home or garage, then you are not going to need much capital to start, but do consider getting insurance cover in case a dog injures itself or your neighbour. Check too with your local Council in case you need permission.

To begin with you could try advertising by putting leaflets through letterboxes in your particular area. In your leaflet, try offering a free gift, such as a flea collar, for every grooming or offer the first grooming at half price. This is to encourage people to try your service. Once you are established you should get business by word of mouth, but you could send reminders to existing customers – a card on the dog's

Business Ideas – A-Z

birthday is a nice idea.

Some people who do dog-grooming, share their fees with established pet shops. The shops act as "spotters" for customers and refer them to the people who do the grooming.

The key factor is contacting dog owners so they are aware your service exists. You could stress that having you do the grooming is a much more pleasant experience for the pet because of your expertise.

Cats present a particular problem as they scratch and may even need to be anaesthetised by a vet.

One good reference book is "The All Breed Dog Grooming Guide" by Kohl & Goldstein.

DRESS HIRE

There is always a need for the hire of expensive dresses for special occasions, be it a wedding or ball. This can be a home-based business though you need a reasonable size of room to store and display the garments. You also need to have a suitable space for clients to be fitted.

Being home-based can be a benefit to customers as they can relax and enjoy themselves and you can arrange appointments in the evenings and week-ends that may suit people who are otherwise working.

The initial purchase cost of the clothes is a drawback as it can cost you £10,000 or possibly much more. Due to space and capital limitations businesses tend to specialise in either wedding gowns and related garments (eg bridesmaids dresses) or they stock only evening dresses and ball gowns. Clients expect a range of accessories to be available and you will need to be able to carry out minor alterations and repairs to garments.

To attract customers you could advertise in the Yellow Pages and by word-of-mouth, so give out a business card to as many people as you know. The business card could carry details on the back – so it becomes a mini promotional leaflet.

With this business (as with any where people come into your home) you should have insurance in case customers injure themselves and your stock needs to be fully insured.

A small, but annoying, downside of this business is when clients phone to make an appointment then don't appear.

DRIVING INSTRUCTOR

This is a popular home-based business but you should only consider it if you are over 21, have a full UK driving licence, have not been disqualified from driving in the past 4 years and you are a calm, patient person and are good at dealing with people. A driving instructor has to cope with clients who can be nervous, irritable, irrational or just slow to learn.

This is not a business that will make you a fortune but it can provide a fairly regular income. One snag is it can take some time to get qualified and start. Another catch is the hours can be long with evening and week-end work.

Having your Approved Driving Instructor's licence and a dual-control car is no guarantee of work. There is usually a lot of competition from other instructors and competing on price alone is not the answer as your running costs will be the same as theirs. You need to compete on the quality of your training and how you handle your customers so they complete their training with you and recommend you to others. Recommendations from clients will provide the majority of your business. Advertising usually yields little response.

ADDRESS

For further information on how to qualify as a Driving Instructor, get the information pack from the Driving Standards Agency, whose address is given at the end of this book.

BSM is a major driving instructor franchise.

EXHIBITION ORGANISER

Exhibitions, Consumer Shows and Trade Shows have today become an important facet of business life. (Here we use the words "Exhibition" and "Shows" interchangeably). For non-retail businesses they provide regional, national and sometimes even international exposure.

There are thousands of shows held around the UK each year. Although some are huge, such as the London International Boat Show, Ideal Home Exhibition or the Motor Show, many are quite small and are likewise organised by small outfits. These smaller shows are often held in hotels around the country.

The work of organising such an event can be home-based because most of the work is done by phone, fax and letter. When you need to meet people (who are mainly potential exhibitors), you will usually have to go to them as you are trying to persuade them to take a stand at your show. This is the tricky bit for if you don't get enough bookings, then the show will not take place.

Running exhibitions can be profitable but you need to be good at organising and have a fairly thick skin. Exhibitors are notorious grumblers and perhaps it is no surprise as exhibiting usually involves considerable travel, accommodation and staff bills in addition to the cost of the stand space. Exhibitors can feel let down by the organisers if too few buyers attend (possibly due to insufficient pre-exhibition publicity) or if any problems are not sorted out quickly.

The exhibition business is always in a state of flux with new exhibitions appearing, others disappearing or being renamed or being sold to other organisers. This turbulence gives an opportunity for a new organiser to step in and run a new and better show.

A "good" show is one which is well attended, participants make good sales and you make a profit.

To be successful in this business you will probably need to know a particular trade very well, have good contacts and feel that you can offer a new exhibition that will fill a gap or compete with an existing show over which there may be dissatisfaction. You could consider running the exhibition in conjunction with a trade association or magazine as that will help your credibility and get the people in.

EXPORTING

Most exporters are manufacturers who are seeking overseas customers, but there is an opportunity for a small home-based export business that does not require you to be a manufacturer. If you lived abroad for many years and still go there on holiday, perhaps to visit relations, then you may have noticed a potential demand for goods that were not available locally but which you could supply from the UK.

In practice you first need to find suitable UK suppliers, get samples and prices, then find an importer in the country concerned who is prepared to order in sufficient quantities. You would arrange for the UK suppliers to truck the goods to your shipper who will consolidate the goods into a container (or part container) and then ship them to the destination country. Here the goods are off-loaded and trucked to the importer's warehouse. You pay the UK suppliers and then invoice the importer, adding a percentage (your profit).

You will need to be familiar with import restrictions, import and export licences, foreign exchange control regulations and shipping details. If you quote prices in Sterling then you need to watch for currency fluctuations that can suddenly make your goods too expensive to sell abroad.

You should be very wary of giving credit, so you need to have buyers pay by documentary credit through a bank. Contact also the DTI's Export Credits Guarantee Department in London (see the end of this book for their address).

This is a business that requires skill, knowledge, sales ability and some capital, but can be both fun and profitable.

FREELANCING

This term can cover a very wide range of professional services. In the publishing world alone it encompasses (in alphabetical order): artists, cartoonists, crossword compilers, designers, editors, illustrators, indexers, photographers, proof-readers, researchers and writers. Many of the people who work in these capacities are members of the NUJ (National Union of Journalists) and a background in the industry is probably essential to have the skills required and the contacts necessary to get work. The NUJ's "Guide to Freelancing" is an excellent guide to what this type of work should pay and gives general advice on contracts. The guide is relevant to all freelancers in publishing, not just NUJ members.

The annual "Writers' & Artists' Yearbook" is an excellent publication and discusses freelance opportunities. The book is available through most bookshops.

Freelancing is not confined to the publishing world as there are, for instance, freelance Public Relations people. But as with publishing, most freelancers will be those who have worked in a given industry prior to setting up on their own. Being "freelance" simply means a professional who sells his or her services to a variety of companies.

ADDRESS

The address of the National Union of Journalists is given at the end of this book.

FURNITURE RESTORATION

There are not many things as satisfying as taking an old chair or sideboard and restoring it to its former glory. Furniture restoration can involve several skills, such as a knowledge of wood and how to repair and polish it, upholstery and caning.

The skills can be learned at many local colleges and you could practice on your own furniture first. It is probably unwise to tackle valuable antique furniture until you are highly skilled. Good advice from one upholsterer is to learn your craft well as nobody will pay for shoddy work. She also suggested you work on one piece at a time. You need good tools and, for upholstery, an industrial sewing machine as domestic ones usually cannot cope with thick fabrics.

Some people repolish wooden furniture without learning the upholstery craft, but this limits your market. Another restoration skill is caning. A lot of old cane furniture is quite reusable provided that the cane part is properly repaired. With a small amount of practice just about anyone can learn to do this properly and find customers. The materials are reasonably easy to obtain and there are a number of books available that show you how to do the work.

With all restoration jobs, note down a client's verbal instructions and let them check and agree the note you have

written so there are no misunderstandings.

If you are good you will soon get business by referral, so ensure you give a couple of business cards to your satisfied customers to hand out to their friends. You could also attach a card neatly to the underside of the piece of furniture so the client can contact you again to restore some other item.

When pricing your work, don't try to undercut everyone else because you will usually find that there is a reason why other people's prices are at that level. There are also customers who assume that if you quote low then you will take shortcuts and it is going to result in a poor job. So competing on price is not the thing to do with a special skill of this kind. Instead stress the quality of your work.

GARDENING

Most people can cut their grass, weed the flower beds and generally potter about in their gardens, but need help for bigger tasks, while others need help with even those basic gardening chores. There is usually a lot of competition to do simple lawn mowing so you will probably need to expand

your service to provide landscaping, planting and maybe even a full gardening service.

However, as usual, you need to do research first. You need to find out who else is offering the service in the area, what they are charging and the range of services that they provide. Talk to their customers and find out how good their services are. Is there a need for a better service or are people looking for other services such as rotovating, laying paths, installing ponds, erecting fences?

Almost certainly you will need transport, ideally a van, but you might instead use a car and trailer. Your van or trailer should carry your trading name – it's a good and free advertisement.

Gardening is, of course, seasonal in the UK so you need to consider how you will survive financially during the long winter months when there will be little to no work to do.

The key factors in this business are calling on customers regularly or having a contract to do, say, a ½ day in their garden each week, plus doing a job well and carefully. In other words, attention to detail is very important. Remember too that people are also paying you for your expertise and general gardening knowledge.

GARMENT CUSTOMISING

If you have some creative ability and an interest in fashion, then there could be a business taking plain garments and creating exclusive items by the application of motifs, hand-painted designs, sequins etc. Your products need not be "up-market" as you could apply designs to T-shirts or teen-age girls' nightwear based on large-sized white T-shirts.

You could apply designs to long cotton nighties, lingerie, evening wear and even bags. Obviously different fabrics will require different paints or processes. Your local textile or art college may be able to help you with technical advice. You might even consider applying the designs by hand screen-printing. If the garment or product you are using has a manufacturer's label then ideally you should have their permission to do this customising.

You need to be clear who your likely customers might be and how you will reach them. Probably the main outlet for

your goods will be shops, particularly fashion boutiques. A catch here is that these small shops usually have relatively small turnovers and will be unable to purchase much from you individually so you will need to sell to a lot of outlets.

Shops will typically want to sell at twice the price you are selling to them, so check your prices are realistic. Try not to sell on consignment (where you don't get paid until after the goods are sold). Operate like a professional business and expect to be treated like any other supplier, for instance being paid in 30 or 60 days.

An alternative to selling through shops is to sell to friends and neighbours. This can be done on a very casual basis or with a bit more organising, by "party plan" selling.

HAIRSTYLIST

Sometimes called a "freelance hairstylist" or "freelance hair-dresser", you would visit the homes of your clients, rather than them having to visit you. Your main advantage over a salon is your customers will tend to be those who have difficulty in visiting a salon because they are very elderly or are invalids or perhaps they have young families to look after.

Check with your local council in case you need to have any licence to operate a hairdressing business. Irrespective of how you plan to operate, you should consider having liability insurance to cover you.

Pricing is very important, because when people have their hair done in their own home, they expect to have it done more cheaply than they could in a salon. But they will still expect it to be as well done as in a salon in their local shopping centre. Although you don't have the high costs of a salon to contend with, you will have to meet the extra cost of running a car.

Some freelance hairstylists have highly specialised businesses. For instance they mainly visit nursing homes, sheltered housing or hospitals. Some are also trained to give beauty therapies.

This is quite a sociable business, unlike many home-based ones that are quite lonely. It is also a cash business, so no bad debts. A downside is the long hours, and you may have to work most evenings.

Word of mouth is the best way to get new customers, so hand a leaflet to everyone you know and all your clients. If you know a freelance beautician who is visiting clients in their homes, perhaps she will also give out your leaflets (in exchange for you telling your clients about her). Newspaper advertising tends to be a waste of money.

HANDYMAN

The DIY boom has encouraged lots of people to try to do things for themselves that they might have had tradesmen do for them in the past. The tougher type of handyman work still needs the assistance of someone who has more than the usual skills of the suburban house owner. Jobs such as putting in stud walls, concreting, damp-proofing, installing skylights, general small building work or repairing doors and windows are ones that most householders do not want to do for themselves. A person with sufficient skills to be a handyman and do these sorts of jobs is always in demand. You may not make a fortune but you should get regular work.

If you have maintained your own home for a number of

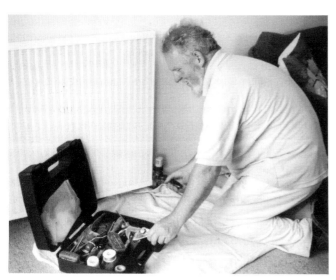

years doing repair and maintenance jobs yourself, you can probably sell those services to others. You may not need any extra training or you may consider attending evening classes to improve your skills. Your clients will mainly be people who are not capable of doing the work as they are elderly or simply do not have the time or inclination.

Very little capital is required to set up this business. If you already have the tools for the jobs that you do around your own home, then few special tools will be required. You may need a ladder or two but you can always hire specialised equipment (eg scaffolding) if you need it for a particular job. Apart from that no additional capital is required, unless you want to purchase a van or estate car.

Unless you are suitably qualified, there are certain jobs you should not do, such as mains wiring, working on gas pipes and appliances or connecting plumbing to sewers.

If you are going to be working on other people's houses, it is really essential to consider having some public liability insurance. You may also consider having personal accident insurance in case you hurt yourself.

It's important to give a quotation in writing for any job over £100 or so and a good idea is to write out your invoice (and get paid) while still on the customer's premises. This not only ensures prompt payment but reduces the incidence of complaints and disputes.

Friendly, prompt service is critical. People who call you will want their work done almost straight away, not in a month's time. Many people who offer this type of work develop a reputation for not turning up at all, so reliability is the first requirement. Also important is the quality of work you do and your attention to the little things like cleaning up the mess after you finish.

HIRING THINGS

If you can afford the capital outlay, there are business opportunities in buying and hiring out things. This usually applies to equipment that is expensive and which potential customers require to use only occasionally. For instance, one couple hires out 4x4 vehicles such as the Discovery and Range Rover. In their rural location there is a good seasonal

The popular Land Rover Discovery, at home on or off-road.

covering, for instance, labelling (with "Best Before" or "Use By" dates), and weights & measures. There are also the bread & flour regulations, sugar & sugar product regulations etc etc. Even what you name your products is controlled. The key to all this is to have a talk with your local Environmental Health Officer (EHO) at the very beginning. Note that EHOs are a source of expertise and can offer advice, they are not simply there to enforce the regulations.

Although the regulations are comprehensive and tough, don't be put off unnecessarily – others manage to cope, so you should too. And remember that most of the regulations relating to food are really quite sensible.

Once you have had a chat with your local EHO and have decided to continue with this idea, then you need to research your market to find out if there is anyone who will actually buy your produce. By speaking to the publicans or shop-keepers you will soon discover if you have a willing market, what they need and what they are prepared to pay.

demand for these vehicles, mainly from visitors. If you don't have your own off-street parking then having vehicles to hire out could give you problems with the local council.

There are, of course, many other things that can be hired out, and another example is holiday caravans on fixed sites (which could be elsewhere in the country).

The main drawback with this business is obvious – the high capital outlay, but a less obvious problem is the risk that you will purchase something and then find the market is insufficient or declining, so careful research is essential.

HOME BAKING

By "Home Baking" we mean the preparation of either pub food or baked products for sale in local shops. In this Business Ideas section of the book we have already touched on the problems of food regulations as they relate to Bed & Breakfast and Catering. It is important to realise that the regulations governing Home Baking are even more stringent than with either B&B or outside catering.

Besides the Food Safety Act, there are a host of regulations

HOUSE RENOVATION

Is this the ultimate home-based business? The house is in fact your business but because it is also your home, under present tax laws, *all the profit could be tax free!*

If you have good DIY skills and you and your family don't mind living continually in a building site, then this is a business to consider. You buy a suitable property in need of renovation, do the necessary work and then sell it. The opportunity exists because a great deal of the housing stock in this country is old and not everyone has the skill or time to do up a house. The profit you make on the sale of the property is also potentially tax free provided the house is your principal private residence and occupied by yourself (but do check the details of this with an accountant beforehand).

Besides needing the necessary building trade skills (and a tolerant family) you should be conversant with local planning regulations and building control requirements.

Finding the right house at the right price may prove tricky as there are other individuals (and builders) who are looking for exactly the same type of properties to do up. Then once you have bought somewhere and completed the renovations,

Business Ideas – A-Z

you may have difficulty in selling it as house sales have been depressed in the UK for some time.

You need to have not only the capital to purchase the building but also enough cash to live on during the year or two it will take to renovate then sell the house. If neither you nor your partner is in employment then getting a mortgage could be very difficult. You might combine a renovation project with some other home-based business.

IMPORTING

To succeed in this business you need to have reliable suppliers and suitable outlets for the goods you plan to import. At one time you could travel to remote parts of the world and buy exotic goods for sale back in the UK or you could journey to low income countries and buy more conventional goods but at relatively low prices. Today the large retail groups send buyers world-wide and there are few corners of the globe they don't reach, so finding saleable goods that are not already available in the UK is more difficult than it used to be.

If you want to start an import business, ideally you would have spent some time in the country where you plan to buy the goods. You would therefore know people you can trust

and you would know the local way of doing things. You may also know the language which is always an advantage to strike the best deal.

Even if you can track down good suppliers abroad, you then need to find enough retailers back here to buy your goods. The UK retail scene is dominated by large chain stores who are relatively impenetrable as they would rather import themselves and miss you out. So you probably need to rely on smaller independent retailers – but they usually buy in small quantities. You could try to meet potential retail buyers by taking a stand at appropriate trade shows (but exhibiting is very expensive).

Any stock you purchase needs to be stored, but if you don't have a suitable (and secure) garage then you could rent space in one of those places that advertise "self-storage" or mini storage.

You will need to be familiar with import licences and to understand shipping details. Problems you may encounter include: suppliers who cheat you, currency exchange rates that shift against you and buyers who are poor payers. But if you can cope with all that, there is still business to be had.

One potentially successful adaptation of this business idea is when you are familiar with a particular UK industry and you get a manufacturer abroad to make up your own designs for importation. If this is substantially better or cheaper than your rivals then you may have a winner – but that is probably getting beyond a simple home-based business.

INDOOR PLANT RENTAL

Providing and maintaining indoor plants for local offices is an idea for people interested in pot plants. Planting has become an important way of decorating offices, banks, builders' show houses, hotels, businesses and restaurants. The people who work in these places do not have the time or perhaps the expertise required to maintain the plants adequately. There is a business opportunity here but competition from other plant rental companies can be tough.

Although you will need to listen to a client's wishes, they will be relying on you for your knowledge of which plants would best suit which locations. You need therefore to have a good knowledge of the plants available and their ability to withstand various conditions of light and temperature. In some cases you might want to use artificial plants as well as natural ones. You will also need to know where you can get plants (usually from nurseries) and you ought to discuss with suppliers getting the plants at trade prices.

Depending upon the number of clients that you have, you will require enough money to finance the purchase of sufficient plants and their containers. You may also need to produce a colour brochure illustrating the various types of plant that you can offer.

For the business to succeed you obviously need to have sufficient customers. When you meet prospective clients, suggest you walk around the premises with them and make recommendations about the kinds of plants that could be placed in each area. Try to inspire their imagination with your description of how attractive their premises could look.

Include in your contract the right to place a small notice on one of your plant pots giving your name and address. You could try a listing in the Yellow Pages and you could also try to advertise in the local newspaper. The editorial staff might even be persuaded to do a short article on your business if you can think of some newsworthy angle. But you will probably gain most by making direct contact with likely customers.

Your business will not always be trouble-free. Plants can get damaged (or stolen) and conditions for the plants can be tricky, eg dark restaurants, temperature changes due to central heating going off over holidays or plants near draughty entrances. This requires you to rotate the plants and make good losses that could reach as much as 40% of your stock per year.

Experience shows that larger offices (such as company headquarters), lawyers' offices, doctors' surgeries and estate agents are often the best accounts to have because they tend to look after the plants much better and have a much cleaner environment.

In setting your charges you should calculate the plant rental and maintenance fees separately because some clients will choose to maintain the plants themselves. Others might want to buy the plants and then just use your maintenance service. The maintenance fee is usually a flat fee that will vary depending on the number of plants being cared for and the distance you need to travel to their premises. If you have a lot of large offices that are fairly close together, then the maintenance fees can be lower. But if it takes an hour to travel from one client to another then you would need to set your charges accordingly.

INTERIOR DESIGN

To be a good interior design consultant requires considerable design skill and flair together with some commercial acumen. Although one might think initially that interior design is mainly to do with home decoration, in fact the major market is in such business places as pubs, offices and hotels.

You need to understand the technicalities and costs of carpet materials, lighting, curtains, wallpaper and paint and where to source all these items. In addition you should have some knowledge of the relevant building regulations and be able to create attractive "visuals" to sell your ideas.

Potential customers will want to see photographs of other work you have done, so to begin with you could stage shots using corners of your home and the homes of friends. Take careful professional photographs. When you complete your first and subsequent jobs, ensure you have several good wide-angle photos taken of each design.

It takes time to make contacts and develop a reputation with this type of business, so it is not ideal if it is likely to be your only source of income. But if you are creative it can be immensely satisfying.

INVENTING

Patents relate to products, processes, mechanisms, materials etc.. To be patentable an invention must be: 1) new; 2) involve an inventive step and 3) be capable of industrial application. It is advisable to contact a Patent Agent (see Yellow Pages) at a very early stage.

In contrast, **Registered Designs** relate to the looks or style of a product and are judged solely by eye. Only the appearance given by an object's actual shape, configuration, pattern or ornament can be protected, not an underlying idea. Again,

Business Ideas – A-Z

Oh no, not another new design of mouse-trap!

you should contact a Patent Agent for more advice at an early stage.

Note you cannot protect a business idea, only something physical.

There are many people who feel they could invent something or perhaps they have an idea that they think could be patented. There is a popular misconception that if you invent something it's a sure way to make your fortune. Sadly, nothing could be further from the truth.

The reality is that if you invent something, even if it is a very good invention with substantial commercial potential, you will usually find British manufacturers you approach will respond with a total lack of interest. Most inventors either have to take their invention abroad to manufacturers in Germany, the United States or Japan, or they end up making the product themselves. This last option does not necessarily require you to set up as a manufacturer because you could use a sub-contractor to make the items for you.

Even having the item made does not solve your problems, for you then need a substantial promotional budget to sell to customers who are generally wary of new things. Of every 10 new product ideas, only one is likely to go into production and of those that do get made, many turn out to be loss makers.

In Britain only about 2% of patents are filed by private individuals, the remainder being filed by companies and government research departments.

Warning: If you wish to apply for a patent or registered design, contact a Patent Agent before publicly disclosing your invention or design as such disclosure forfeits your protection.

ADDRESS

The Patent Office has several free booklets. Its address is given at the end of this book.

JAM MAKING

There is always a market for bottles of jam sold as gift items, usually to tourists. As a gift item its price need not compete with the mass-produced confections available in supermarkets, but the design of the packaging is vital. So an interesting shape of bottle, attractive lid and label are all essential. Ideally the ingredients could be slightly unusual, preferably with some local connection if that is possible.

If you are interested in this business idea you probably already bottle jam for your own consumption but it is important to realise that as you cross the threshold from domestic to commercial cooking, then a huge range of regulations suddenly come into play. Besides the Food Safety Act, there are regulations covering, for instance, labelling (with "Best Before" or "Use By" dates), weights & measures and the sugar & sugar product regulations, just for starters. Even what you call your products is controlled. The key to all this is to have a talk with your local Environmental Health Officer (EHO) at the very beginning. EHOs are a useful source of expertise, they are not simply there to enforce the many regulations.

Although the regulations are comprehensive and tough, don't be put off unnecessarily – others manage to cope, so you should too. And remember that most of the regulations relating to food are really quite sensible.

Once you have crossed that barrier, the main problem, as always, is finding sufficient outlets for your produce and this will probably be the limiting factor on your business. Typical outlets will be those shops frequented by tourists. Remember that includes local grocery stores in addition to gift shops.

First, look around shops to see if they already sell similar jams, who makes them and what price they are selling for. You could make sample bottles of your own jams, work out a price and then discuss it with the manager or manageress of each shop. You will soon discover if there is a market for your produce. If it depends on tourists it will be seasonal though you may find a proportion sell to local customers too.

JEWELLERY MAKING

You may have learned to make jewellery at Art College or it may have been a hobby or it is just something you want to learn to do. Assuming you have some design talent and the necessary technical skills, then sourcing the component parts or raw materials will take some time and research.

You could make relatively affordable costume jewellery or you could work in precious metals with semi-precious stones. It all depends on your training and skills. You can buy stones already polished and various lengths of chains and settings ready for your assembly. Note too the provisions of the Hallmarking Act 1973 (details from Trading Standards).

However the key to making a profit is getting the jewellery into the right outlets. You have two choices – you could wholesale to shops or you could sell through party plan. Costume jewellery is cheap to buy and retailers will want a minimum 100% mark-up, often much more, so this will reduce your profit margin rather dramatically and encourage you to consider selling it direct through party plan. Party plan selling is discussed in more detail in a later chapter entitled **Business Ideas – Direct Selling**. A useful niche is individual orders where customers are trying to match colours with an outfit for a special occasion.

KNITTING

Knitting is a popular pastime and can provide useful income (albeit usually part-time). There is a market for both machine and hand knitted garments, though there are snags. If you add up how long you take to complete a garment then you may find that the return in terms of £/hour is likely to be low. But the process can be speeded up, for instance by using a linker to sew-up the garments.

The time to produce a garment can be divided roughly into three parts: one third to plan, measure, check tensions and do size calculations; one third to knit and the last third to finish off the garment.

If you try selling through retail outlets, the return on your labour will be even lower and they may only buy "on consignment" (where they don't pay you until the garment is sold), but at least they are providing a display for your goods. You make a better return if you can sell direct to customers by making to order for friends and then their friends. You could also consider taking a small stand at craft fairs. It helps if you can design your own garments, patterns or decorations. For for instance you might design a boy's sweater with his favourite toy illustrated on the front. This potentially commands a premium price (if the designs are any good).

Overall, knitting is a satisfying, though solitary, type of business, but one word of caution – if, as a novice, you think you just have to buy a knitting machine and start producing saleable garments, then think again! Your articles should look *hand made*, not *home made!*

MAGAZINE PUBLISHING

There are "consumer" magazines that you find in newsagents, "trade" magazines that are circulated to people in a specific trade and "private subscription" magazines on special interest subjects that are subscribed to by individuals.

To break into the consumer market is difficult due to the distribution to newsagents being controlled by a small number of distributors and shelf space in newsagents being at a premium. It is normally a very costly exercise and requires resources greater than most home-based businesses can muster.

In contrast, the other two areas (trade and private subscription) could certainly be done from home and are potentially lucrative.

Business Ideas – A-Z

Trade "mags" can generate income from advertising and subscriptions. Although the circulation of a trade magazine is much smaller than a consumer mag, the *buying power* of the readers can be large and that is attractive to advertisers. Many publishers choose to distribute their magazines free and rely solely on advertising revenue. This decision is usually because the advertisers are only interested if the publication has a high penetration of its market and a magazine requiring subscriptions may attract fewer readers. In practice some magazines distribute some copies free and others on subscription.

With private circulation magazines, the revenue is from both advertising and subscription but the readers buying power is likely to be small and advertising revenue will therefore usually be much less than a trade magazine.

To succeed in magazine publishing you need to have in-depth knowledge of the subject covered and an ability to sell advertising. It would also help if you can write authoritatively on the subject as relying on freelance writers will erode profits.

MINI GLOSSARY FOR PUBLISHERS

ABC   Means a mag's circulation has been officially audited.

Assembly   Multipage printing requires a number of sheets of film to be assembled accurately before printing can begin.

Bleed   This is where eg a photo goes off the edge of the paper.

Circulation   The number of copies you sell or distribute. The "readership" is likely to be several times that figure.

Half Tone   Black & white photos or illustrations which include shades of grey that need "screening" (see below).

Imposition   Refers to the position of pages on the assembly film so pages appear in correct sequence when printed and folded.

Laminating   Puts a glossy surface on the magazine's cover. An alternative is "varnishing".

Pagination   The number or numbering of pages in an issue.

Perfecting   A binding process that gives a squared-off spine. The alternative is "saddle-stitching" with wire staples.

Piece   Journalist slang for an article. Also called "copy".

Rate Card   A leaflet with advertising rates, details of circulation, the deadlines for adverts for each issue and technical details.

Screening   This photo process converts grey shades in a black & white photo into black dots so it can be printed.

Separations   To print colour photos or illustrations you need 4 sheets of film, called separations or "seps".

Tranny   Slang for a colour transparency. A "dupe tranny" is a duplicate or copy of a colour transparency.

You need to learn about magazine production and distribution and ideally you should be able to design and typeset the magazine yourself – using desktop publishing.

Advertisers don't pay until well after an issue is published and subscribers are unlikely to pay until you have an issue to sell, so you need to be able to finance the first issue. A big problem is that advertisers (or their Ad Agencies) are notoriously bad payers so you can be producing your second or even third magazine while still chasing late-payers from the first issue. This increases the start-up capital you require.

You also have the setting up costs of your home-based office. This requires a powerful PC or Mac computer and fax as a minimum. A small photocopier is also very useful. In addition, to get any advertising for the first issue you will almost certainly have to produce a "rate card" and a mock-up magazine to show to potential advertisers. A big challenge is the need to acquire or create your initial mailing list.

There is a lot of competition with magazines. Look at the directory called BRAD in any main library. This lists virtually all magazines produced in Britain. It also gives details of their advertising rates and circulations (though many publications have no independently verified circulation figures).

Other hassles include printing and distribution problems. Deadlines can be very stressful. Despite all those problems, good magazines can and are produced by home-based businesses and it is very satisfying to create a publication that is well respected by its readers.

MANUFACTURER'S AGENT

If you enjoy sales work and don't mind a lot of travelling and being away from home then this could interest you. There is always a demand for agents, but it's hard work and can be unrewarding financially until you find the right company with good "lines" to sell. Ideally you would already have good experience of the particular industry you plan to work in.

An agent visits shops (or offices or whatever) and tries to make sales on behalf of a manufacturer. The agent carries samples and order pads (supplied free) and will hope to write the orders there and then. The manufacturer is then responsible for delivering the goods, invoicing the customer and collecting the dues. The agent then gets commission on those sales (10%-15% of the invoice total, excluding any VAT, is typical in many industries).

It is vital to have a written Agreement that has been checked by your solicitor. The Agreement will cover a wide range of matters, including the following: a) *Commission* The rate to be paid and when it will be paid; b) *Territory* The area in which the agent can operate and if all sales made in that area earn commission even if a customer orders direct from the manufacturer (such commission is normal); c) *Products* The products or product groups that the agent will sell; d) *Authority* The agent's authority (if any) to negotiate different prices/delivery terms etc and e) *Termination* The period of notice required by either side to end the Agreement.

A good manufacturer will train an agent so he or she is familiar with their products and sales techniques and should also provide a list of existing and potential customers with contact names. Most agents represent several companies whose goods are not in competition with each other but have the same customers.

Problems you may encounter include slow paying (or worse, non-payment) by your company; the company may not deliver the goods; the commission you earn can be gobbled up by your travel costs and if selling to shops, you find that most retail chains purchase centrally.

Manufacturers seeking agents advertise in their trade press and often put up cards "AGENTS WANTED" at trade shows.

ADDRESS There are two organisations that may help you – the Manufacturers' Agents' Association and the British Agents Register. Their addresses are given at the end of this book.

MINI-CAB HIRE

Outside London these are also called Private Hire Cars. Unlike taxis, a mini-cab doesn't usually have a meter and cannot just pick up a "fare" from the street or sit in a taxi rank. Mini-cabs have to be booked by phone or at a mini-cab office. The licensing requirements for mini-cabs varies around the country. Ask your local authority what rules apply

to your area. Three requirements that are common to all are: 1) you need to be fully covered with "hire and reward" insurance; 2) your car must be roadworthy and 3) you must have a full driving licence.

A problem facing most mini-cab drivers is that profit margins are slim and there is a lot of competition. This is not a business that is likely to make you rich but it could provide some extra income. It usually involves long hours.

As with any business idea you need to fully research the likely demand. In this case find out how many mini-cabs are operating in your area, what they tend to charge and how much work they are getting.

Ideally you want to find yourself a niche, such as becoming the preferred "taxi" service for a large company, hospital or similar. Being reliable (i.e. turning up on time when booked), keeping the interior of your car spotless and treating your customers properly should all help you gain custom at your competitors' expense.

PAINTING & DECORATING

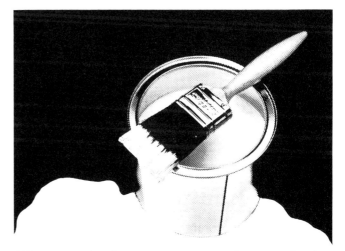

Although your local newspaper may contain many advertisements by other painters and decorators, there are always opportunities for people who are good and quick at this work and who can provide sensible quotations. Interior decorating is a year-round business though outside painting can be limited by the weather. Remember that not only do homes need painting but so do offices and shops. Besides painting and wall-papering you could also consider doing wall tiling of kitchens and bathrooms.

Obviously you need the normal professional skills for painting and for decorating. Courses at local colleges are available but are no substitute for practical experience. If you have decorated your own home over a number of years, then you probably have enough skills, though you may still wish to take some further training.

You will require all the tools of the trade and as you will need long ladders you will probably need a car with a roof rack or a van. As you are working in other people's homes or business premises you should consider taking out adequate insurance to cover you if you accidentally damage their property.

The absolutely critical factors in this business are the quality of the finished job and your price. It is also important that you lay down sheets and covers to protect the client's carpets and furniture, and that you tidy up properly at the end of the job. If you do a good job in someone's home, then you can be certain that you will get other work by recommendation, so leave a few business cards.

PET BREEDING

If you have a genuine love of animals, have the necessary knowledge, and your home is suitable, then this business idea might be of interest. But do consider the impact on your domestic life as caring for animals is a full-time, 7 days-a-week, 365 days-a-year commitment.

Your first decision is what to breed. Apart from the obvious pedigree dogs and cats, there are many other options: birds, particularly budgerigars and parrots; tropical and other ornamental fish; guinea pigs and hamsters; rabbits and even horses, if you have sufficient space. Note that some "wild" animals are classed as dangerous and you would need a licence just to keep them.

At an early stage of your planning, find out from your local council what their regulations are, as they could be onerous.

For instance, you usually need a licence if you plan to breed dogs and you may need to apply for planning permission. There may also be legal limitations imposed by the terms of ownership of your house, so check with a solicitor. Your local vet is another person you should talk to.

Research the proposal thoroughly and find out all you can about the breeding of the animal concerned. Your research should include a study of the market for that animal. Various breeds of dogs, for example, come and go in popularity. Having decided what you are going to breed, seek advice from the various societies dedicated to those animals. Pedigree animals are often sold through shows and breeder's magazines.

Pricing must be based on what are existing market rates. Following up advertisements by other breeders is the best way to work out your prices. Note there is little point in trying to undercut your opposition as most people do not buy on price alone.

PHOTOGRAPHY/VIDEO

Many people are interested in photography or video. There are over a thousand photographic clubs around the country. Anyone can push the shutter on a camera but it takes a special talent to combine the eye of an artist with the skills of

Hard at work in the darkroom!

a business person. Successful photographers are those who combine what they have learned from photography classes with experience and practice. Most will advise that you go on taking additional training after your business begins. The field is overrun with people who believe that they know enough to go into the photography business. So your photography has to be better than the others and you need to be able to promote and market yourself too. There are several areas in which you can specialise:

Wedding photography This is a popular specialisation. As you only get one chance to take the photos, it is a big responsibility and you should look at the location in advance. You should also be aware of any special customs and traditions that the family may have. You should not intrude too much in what is going on, and you should dress just like any other guest. Remember to have a back-up camera and lighting. Brides and grooms buy wedding albums but if you can sell parents albums as well by getting a number of shots with the parents in them, then that adds to the profit.

Portrait photography This is another specialisation and is usually portraits of children or family groups. It is a difficult area, but getting good photographs of babies and children is very rewarding both financially and in terms of professional pride. And don't forget *School photography* with the class and team shot or sports day winners.

Other, less common areas of specialisation, include: the quality reproduction of prized photos; aerial photography; household contents photography (for insurance purposes); framed photo art (where a family portrait can be enhanced to look like an oil painting) and framed photographs (where artistic photos are suitably framed, signed by the photographer and sold as a numbered limited edition).

A colleague of ours creates postcards from his photos but the investment is significant and much time and effort is needed visiting shops and persuading them to stock the cards. You then need to revisit regularly to keep the "spinners" stocked (and to chase slow paying retailers). Another use of your photos is to turn them into books or calendars, but that is best done in conjunction with an established book or calendar publisher. Another couple we know took professional quality transparencies while on exotic holidays around the world. They are now considering setting up a photo library offering the use of these shots to magazines and design studios.

Some photographers are used by the local press but that is a difficult market to break into, though there may be more opportunity to take photos for estate agents and those second-hand car publications that feature a photo of each car for sale.

The arrival of video has widened the market, especially as the cost of broadcast standard cameras and editing equipment has fallen, but making money out of doing video work is again not that easy. Some enterprising photographers are taking videos of expensive properties on behalf of estate agents, while others visit popular holiday locations and take a travel film for duplication and sale. Such films can include advertising by local hotels and tourist attractions to help cover the costs.

PICTURE FRAMING

There is a steady market for framing pictures but there is also quite a lot of competition from other picture framers, many of whom have shops that give them a higher profile than a home-based business. However, they have higher overheads too, and that should give you a price advantage.

Many framers started work just after completing a course or they teach themselves from books and by practice. Besides framing pictures that people bring you, you could also buy prints, antique or modern, frame them and sell them as finished pictures.

The capital required for stock and equipment is not particularly great but you need a reasonably large place to work – such as a garage. You can store the long lengths of mouldings in the garage ceiling. It is possible to spend a fortune stocking the various mouldings, but you may be able to simply have sample corners to show to customers and then purchase the mouldings you need from a wholesaler.

Advertising this business is difficult and likely to give poor returns. It is better to make direct contact with people who are likely to use your service. You might keep in touch with galleries, art societies, photographic clubs, commercial photographers, instant print shops and art classes. Just try thinking of all the things that can be framed and put up on the wall. Seeking out these sources of customers is one of the key

Business Ideas – A-Z

factors to success. Repeat orders and recommendation by word-of-mouth are other essential factors.

To stay in business you will need to please your clients and look after their treasures. Many are valuable and if you damage them you could be sued for substantial amounts of money, so you need to be very careful with the jobs that you are given and be properly insured.

PLANT NURSERY

If your garden is big enough you might consider growing some small cash crops. Depending on the situation of your garden, whether you have a greenhouse or not, and where you are located in the country, you could grow herbs, heathers, alpines etc.

Naturally what you grow will dictate how you sell your produce. If you are growing herbs, you could try selling them to shops and possibly restaurants. The most popular herbs are likely to be those used for cooking.

With small plants such as heathers you might sell direct to people or via garden centres. In some parts of the country you may find you can sell small plants through unusual outlets, for instance heather sold at petrol filling stations and in gift shops in the Highlands of Scotland. If you live at the side of a main road you might attract passing trade (though check your local Council approves).

It may pay to specialise and your local horticultural college is an invaluable source of practical knowledge.

Although small producers selling plants locally are generally exempt from regulations, there are some laws mainly to avoid the risk of spreading plant diseases. Hence anyone planning to set up a nursery should seek guidance from their local area office of the Ministry of Agriculture.

PUBLISHING PRINTS

If you have artistic talent combined with the necessary commercial flair, this can be a profitable business. If you are a good enough artist you could create the originals yourself, otherwise you would need to commission artists to do the work (and then agree what royalty to pay them). Although artists can sell their originals, a better way to exploit the full commercial potential may be to have prints made. In this case your business will comprise some artistic work but will mainly consist of finding and stocking retail outlets for your prints.

If your subject is essentially tourist orientated then you need to seek shops in the area(s) concerned. You will soon discover that shops in one area will not stock landscapes of another area as they want local views and scenes, so you will need to have many different prints. It would not be economical to revisit your outlets in person each time you want to re-stock them so you need to make follow-on sales by phone every month or so. Then visit them again when you have something new to show them.

It is probably a good idea to specialise in a particular subject area so that you eventually get a reputation, eg it could be prints of landscapes, aviation, motorsport, shipping, railways, animals etc. You could use the same image on a variety of products, eg calendars, greetings cards and books, to build up a range. This may require the image to be reduced or "cropped" to a different shape.

If your forte is a specialist subject such as aircraft, then there may be galleries and mail order print firms that deal with that topic. You could also consider advertising in appropriate magazines.

To increase your profit return, you could produce signed and numbered limited editions of 300-500 or so prints as these can command a higher price than unnumbered prints.

SCREEN PRINTING TEXTILES

Sometimes called "silk-screen printing" as the screens were once made of silk, for a home-based business you will probably be limited to screen printing textiles by hand.

A visit to any craft or gift shop will reveal a large number of screen printed goods, although many will be machine printed. The actual technical process of hand screen printing of textiles is relatively straightforward and the basics could be learned on a short college course. It's vital that the designs to be printed are really good.

You will need sufficient capital to buy or make your own printing table and exposure unit plus the initial materials, screens and inks. You may also need a sewing machine to make up or finish your goods.

Assuming you can produce good commercial designs and print them satisfactorily the main problem is finding outlets for your goods. The competition is stiff and the market expects multi-coloured prints that are often done by machine as they are more difficult and time consuming to do by hand. As shops are likely to be your main outlets, early discussions with them, perhaps showing them your artwork, will help you decide if a big enough market exists.

Screen printing on T-shirts and fashion garments are other potential markets – see GARMENT CUSTOMISING.

ADT Auctions have 25 auction centres around the country.

SECOND-HAND CAR SALES

Half the households in Britain own a car, nearly a fifth own two or more and each year millions of second-hand cars are sold. So the market is huge, but equally so is the competition. Anyone wanting to buy a used car can buy one privately or at an auction or from a garage forecourt or a franchised dealer or from a second-hand car dealer.

These days buyers seek assurances regarding a car's history and they demand good warranties. They may also require finance to help them purchase the car they want. While a new-start business operating from home can feasibly offer all this, they will tend to have less credibility. However the home-based business has two major advantages: 1) low overheads (which translates into lower priced cars) and 2) the opportunity of providing a really personal service.

Before considering this business you need to have a very sound and thorough knowledge of cars and how auctions work (which will probably be your main source of cars). If you know someone already in the trade who is willing to give you some advice, so much the better. You will also need to consider if Planning Permission is required and talk to your local Trading Standards Officer. As you are dealing in second-hand goods you will probably need a trader's licence

from your local authority. If your turnover is likely to exceed the VAT threshold, then you should also consult HM Customs & Excise. There is a special VAT scheme for second-hand cars.

Some tips to help you succeed: write good adverts that are different (remember your adverts must be accurate and show you are a trader); consider specialising (eg become the person for used Fiestas or Metros etc) and keep a stock book giving full details of all cars you buy and sell.

Perhaps as many as one third of all used cars have some sort of "hidden history". One company, HPI Equifax, provides information on cars over the phone (for a fee).

 ADDRESS The address of HPI Equifax and the head office of ADT Auctions Ltd are both given at the end of this book.

SECRETARIAL SERVICES

If you are a reasonably good typist and have good inter-personal skills, a secretarial service is a good business to run from home. Expenses can be very low and there is scope to make some useful profit.

You can provide a variety of services, not just the typing of letters. For instance you could do CVs for people who are applying for jobs; provide an editing service to correct written material; type theses, essays and manuscripts; type labels; or layout and type newsletters. It is a very broad field and most people who run this type of business from home find that they are kept fairly busy once they have built up their contacts.

Versatility and adaptability are essential requirements so that you can match the needs of your different clients. You must also be reliable and capable of handling confidential documents.

Before starting you should consider using a business name. If you are going to be serious about the business, a snappy name will help promote your service. You may also need to set down some strict business hours, otherwise you will find that clients will be calling at all hours of the day and night. You might consider having an answering machine to maintain your established hours.

The skills required are fairly obvious – you need to be able to type and these days you need a word processor or, better still, a computer with a word-processing software package and be able to use that well enough to be able to set out quite complicated documents. Some of the material that you get may already be on computer disk in which case your machine would probably need to be able to cope with both 3½ and 5¼ inch size diskettes. The computer hardware is relatively cheap but if you are buying do ensure you get good advice from an *unbiased* person (preferably not the computer sales people). You will need a printer that can produce top quality documents, probably a bubble-jet, ink-jet or laser printer rather than a dot matrix printer.

You need to be conversant with one or more of the better known word processing packages, such as WordPerfect, WordStar or Word for Windows. Then you can advertise that you can use those packages and this will help to attract more clients.

To get your initial business, contact everyone you know in a management position in business or who runs their own business locally. You could also ask your local Enterprise Agency to let it be known that you can provide this service for new businesses who perhaps do not yet need a full-time secretary but who could do with your help. If you had a photocopier or fax machine you could provide those extra services for your clients.

Although you may be able to do most of your work at home, there may also be opportunities to provide temporary cover in the workplace of some of your clients. This tends to be either to cover staff sickness or at holiday time, which could be inconvenient for you. These firms will use you rather than a temp agency because you are probably cheaper and they already know you.

SEWING (ALTERATIONS & DRESSMAKING)

There was a time when many women had sewing machines and could sew. That is no longer the case and many simply don't have the time to do it anyway. There is therefore a demand for people who can do alterations or make up clothes from patterns.

A sewing machine can be a fairly costly item, however good second-hand machines can be bought instead. You will need other dressmaking bits and pieces but this outlay can usually be recovered very quickly. For a special occasion dress, you could charge around £60 to £75 to make it from a pattern (excluding the material). If other services, such as design or drafting of the pattern, were required there would be extra charges. For wedding dresses and other major jobs, charges could start at around £100. Doing alterations (such as letting out trousers and skirts) can make additional money and there are curtains and chair covers to be made too. So overall you could grow this into a full-time business.

One big attraction is that the work can be done in your own time, whenever you feel like it, though you may find that the business tends to be seasonal. Before Christmas you will have a lot of special jobs to do as people get dresses for parties.

You might want to specialise in one area perhaps making wedding dresses or garments for customers who are an unusual size or shape.

Advertising can be done in a number of ways. You can put a card in a local shop window or leave leaflets with local dry-cleaners and in shops that sell fabrics. Word of mouth is the best way of people getting to know about you and in time you should build up a good solid customer base with lots of repeat business if you treat your customers well.

A useful spin-off is you could run sewing classes that should help to build your reputation as an expert and will also bring you in a number of customers. Running the classes should not conflict with your business as your students are unlikely to have the time or skill to compete with you and the market demand can generally absorb other people doing sewing in any area.

There is more information on running classes in the later chapter **Business Ideas – Teaching**, on page 104.

SOFTWARE WRITING

As computers become increasingly powerful and widespread in their use, people are finding new applications for them. In addition, the almost explosive growth of the Internet has provided new opportunities. All this has created a major, and rapidly expanding, market for software. Although the large software companies dominate the market with programs for most standard applications, there is a market for more specialised programs.

One advantage of writing such programs for niche markets is you can usually, but not always, charge a premium price for it, which will compensate for the fact that you are unlikely to sell many units (in comparison with the big boys).

This is an ideal business to run from home provided you are completely computer literate, own a relatively powerful PC or Mac and enjoy this solitary type of work. But you still need the business acumen to sell your output.

Once you have created your program and selected users have tested samples, then you need to think of the packaging and reproduction of copies. Designing and producing the packaging and manual will take time and money. Most software (other than some shareware) is sold in cartons with full colour printing – this is very expensive to produce and there are no short-cuts if you are trying to sell your programs through retail outlets.

After you have printed the packaging and manual, then your real task is to find buyers. You have several options – if the program is of general interest you could try to wholesale it through computer software dealers. The main problem being that they are very choosy as to what they stock and are

unlikely to buy a new program from an unknown company. If the program is very specialised you could try advertising in appropriate magazines and do direct sales. Alternatively you could offer the program as shareware, which is a popular option for small software houses and certainly one to consider.

A major drawback with this business idea is the long lead time between starting to write the software and actually getting any money back. Ideally you need to combine it with other computer-based work to give you some early income.

ADDRESS

The addresses of shareware distributors in the UK are given at the end of this book.

SPECIALISED TOURS

If you enjoy being an organiser, have a particular cultural or sporting interest, can relate to all types of people, and are fanatical about details, then you might consider arranging specialised tours. These tours could be, for example, of mediaeval castles, the best art galleries of England, the great

Tours of British golf courses are popular with visitors.

Business Ideas – A-Z

botanical gardens of Britain, the whisky distilleries of Scotland or the historical World War 2 sites in Europe. Your tours could include sports activities, so you might, for example, run tours of the top golf courses.

There are two aspects to this business. First you need to create a tour itinerary that is irresistible to its target audience and second you need to track down those people who might want to go on your tour. If your customers are coming from abroad, eg North Americans who wish to play on each of several famous golf courses, then it would help to have good contacts in golfing circles in North America. In contrast, if you were planning to run tours of WW2 battlefields in Europe then your customers could come from a number of countries and you would need to target your advertising appropriately.

Tying up contracts with hotels, restaurants and bus companies needs some knowledge of contract law and the ability to read and understand the inevitable "small print".

This business idea is really as wide as your imagination and energy permits. Although it is an area of growth, you do need to be completely professional in its execution.

TRAINING COURSES or SEMINAR ORGANISER

There are two quite different business opportunities here – one that targets businesses and another that targets the general public.

Businesses   As employers become more conscious of the need for their staff to have up-to-date skills and knowledge, they find that they have to spend money on staff training. Thus demand grows for other businesses to provide the necessary training courses and seminars. There is scope for people who can organise these, even if they do not personally have the skills to present the information.

You could think of a subject which you consider will be of interest, find suitable speakers and a venue and then advertise or direct mail companies to get people to attend. Alternatively you could approach organisations with training budgets, such as the TECs (LECs in Scotland), and produce a course which meets their requirements. See page 19 for information on TECs and LECs and how to contact them. Some companies may wish you to run a course "in- house" for just the employees of their firm.

It's essential you use professional speakers or you will let the whole event down badly. You may find someone who is an expert in their field but a useless speaker; what you need is someone who is both an expert *and* a good speaker.

No formal qualifications are required to be an organiser but a knowledge of what happens on training courses and seminars and how other people have managed them is essential.

Little capital is required unless you are bringing a high-profile speaker from overseas. Some of the venues and catering services that you might want to use may require an advance deposit from you when you book.

The key factor is the quality of the courses/seminars that you organise. Quality means all parts of the seminar: the speakers, the venue, the food, the surroundings that you provide, the pleasantness of the whole experience for the participants and the perceived value to their businesses. Much of this will rely on your organisational skills.

One caution: if you are asked to organise an event on behalf of a company, read the small print of the contract carefully because you could end up paying for the venue and food if they suddenly cancel the event.

General Public   So far we have only talked about business clients but there is another group who are interested in courses and that is individuals who wish to learn a new craft, improve their technical skills or gain some qualification.

Courses can be run in cookery, painting, antiques, interior design . . . to name just a few that are regularly advertised. Courses often take place over a week-end or during a week's break in some pleasant location. This business is discussed in more detail in the chapter **Business Ideas – Teaching.**

TRANSLATION SERVICE

If you are fluent in another language, this is a business option you may like to consider. If you can translate technical or medical text or you can speak an unusual language, you can command a premium. Your work could include translating business documents and acting as interpreter for visitors from overseas.

To get work you could contact the commercial attaché at the London embassy or consulate of the country concerned to offer your services. Your local Chamber of Commerce may also know of British companies who are trading or wish to trade with that country.

You might also inform the British commercial attaché in the country concerned that you can help firms with their communications – you provide a fax number for the firms to send you their faxes which you then translate and fax on, in English.

You could use your linguistic skills in other ways, for instance by giving lessons to individuals, to groups of company employees or through evening classes at College. One interesting adaptation of this is to give one-to-one language instruction by phone to busy executives.

If you have lived for some time in the country concerned you might also be able to provide background knowledge and contacts to British companies who want to export there.

So your foreign language and country knowledge can be used in a number of profitable ways.

MINI GLOSSARY OF TYPESETTING & DTP

Camera Ready Artwork   Text, drawings etc prepared to a final state so they look exactly as they will appear on the final page.

Dpi   Dots per inch. A measure of the resolution or quality you can get from a printer or scanner.

Fonts   A set of one typeface.

Gsm   Grams/square metre. Describes the weight of paper.

Keyline   A line around a box or illustration.

Leading   The space between lines of text – measured in points.

Line Drawings   Graphs or sketches with only black lines.

Mono   Monotone, i.e. one colour, usually black.

Origination   A general term to describe the preparation of camera ready artwork.

Point   A printer's unit of measurement. 1 point = 0.3515mm.

Process Colours   Magenta, cyan and yellow are called process colours. Combined with black they can reproduce full colour.

Reverse Out   The text on page 57 is reversed out of the grey background tint.

Tints   The tint of black in this box or on page 57 are examples.

Typefaces   The different styles of print. There are many hundreds in use. This book is typeset in Korinna.

Weight   The thickness of a line, usually measured in points.

TYPESETTING (DESKTOP PUBLISHING)

Desktop publishing (DTP) has made great inroads into the publishing and printing world. Work which used to require bulky typesetting machines and messy inks is now done using little more than a desktop computer and a laser printer. Although competition has forced trade typesetting charges down, there is still work to be had, particularly if you can produce reliable and accurate work quickly. You can also gain an advantage by offering additional services such as graphics and image scanning.

DTP used to have a bad name as pages were output using low definition (300dpi) laser printers that were not really suitable for professional work, but today you can purchase laser printers with a much higher definition or you can output your work through an imagesetter on a bureau basis. This latter approach gives you the best results.

To be able to do DTP you need three essential pieces of equipment – a reasonably powerful computer, a laser printer and some desktop publishing software. You must decide whether to have a PC computer or a Mac. Historically the Mac was the preferred machine though today there is little to choose between the two and they can both run the same DTP software (such as PageMaker, Quark or Ventura). Having the right equipment is one thing, being able to use it properly is another! Despite what the software sellers might claim, to use any of these highly sophisticated programs on a commercial basis will take both time and patience. Basic computer skills too are essential.

Once you have mastered the skills, the next challenge is to get work. You could try large printers (who although they have their own typesetting departments, may have more work than they can cope with). You could also try high street instant printers. Book publishers are another market. In contrast, magazine publishers will usually require you to be able to work in colour and have more design capability.

Publishers tend to be Mac computer based. You could combine a graphics design business with your typesetting so that you are able to provide a wider range of services.

As with any service, you need to know exactly what your competitors are charging. If you overcharge you will get very little business but if you undercharge you will be working for very little profit.

One problem with typesetting is the different typeface fonts. You will need many and they can be quite costly. Another problem (like many businesses) is poor payers.

WINE SALES

If you are a wine buff, know Oz Clarke's books from cover to cover, think you can buy wine wholesale and have a lot of friends who are wine drinkers then you might consider this business idea. It works by direct selling with you visiting prospective buyers, offering wine tasting then selling them a minimum of one case. You hope to get repeat business from them and in addition widen your client base by perhaps offering a free (good) bottle of wine for every introduction that leads to a sale.

Although there is plenty of competition from super-markets, wine shops, wine clubs and wine by mail order, your overheads are low and a lot then depends on your ability to select good wines and make sales.

Storing liquor is a problem as insurers will require a high level of security and will also charge big premiums. You could minimise stock holding by only ordering from your suppliers when you have orders to fulfill. You may need to store the liquor in a warehouse rather than at home.

When you are ready to despatch an order, consider delivering it in person, by appointment. This would give you an opportunity to provide a wine tasting to take an order for delivery the following month when you could repeat the whole process.

Before you get carried away with the idea of combining an enjoyable pastime with a business, find out who else is doing this and be wary of promises by friends who say they will buy lots of wine from you when you start. You should also ask your local authority if there is any need for a licence ■

Business Ideas – A-Z

Some Other Business Ideas . . . .

Aerobics Classes　If you know what you are doing, you could organise aerobics classes (usually held in a local hall, not your own home). Ensure you are fully insured.

Agencies　You could set up an agency for any one of a range of specialised services, for example: au pairs, nannies, cleaners, nurses etc. Note you will probably need a licence – see the back of this book for the address of the Employment Agencies Licensing Office.

Antique Dealing　This is one business where you need to know your subject matter well or you will be taken advantage of very quickly by other traders. You are probably best to specialise in one niche area. You could start home-based but you may have to move to retail premises as your business grows. You may need a licence – speak to your local Council.

Cake Making　There is always a market for elaborate cakes for special occasions. Speak to your local Environmental Health Officer about the relevant regulations long before you start.

Calligraphy　Beautiful calligraphy appeals to many people and there is a market for this on certificates, menus, posters, special invitations and letterheads. It may be difficult finding sufficient customers to generate an adequate income. You could try approaching High Street instant print shops.

Car Boot Sales　First check out the regular sites where these sales are held. A big advantage is the very low overheads but a disadvantage is you can usually only sell cheap items, typically under £10, better if much less. Some sites don't allow new goods to be sold. Check with your local Council if you need a traders licence.

Car Valeting　Most people tend to either valet their own cars or just let them get dirty, so the potential market is limited. However, cars usually need valeting before they are sold so you could offer this service to private sellers and car dealers.

Flat Letting　In this business you handle the letting of other people's flats (or houses). It's mainly relevant if you live in a large town or city where there is a need for temporary accommodation, eg London, any university city or a tourist location. Get a solicitor to draft the contract you need for the owner and the different contract you need for the tenant. Ensure you are properly insured too.

House Minding　This involves looking after other people's homes when they are away on holiday or working abroad. You might forward their mail, cut the grass and water the plants. Ensure you are properly insured.

House Signs　If you are good at woodworking, enamelling, cold casting or some other appropriate skill, there is a market for decorative house and business nameplates.

Ironing Service　We all complain about doing this chore, and there are some small businesses who offer this service, but it's not a business that would appeal to everyone.

Mobile Mechanic　This could interest the keen DIY car person. As a mobile mechanic you could service or repair customer's cars at their homes (or places of work), thereby avoiding the planning constraints on doing this type of work at your own home.

Business Ideas – A-Z

Some Other Business Ideas (continued) . . . .

Philately

Good fun, but to make any money requires a lot of knowledge of the trade and some capital to build up stock to sell. The twice yearly STAMPEX Trade Fair in London would be worth a visit. Contact the Philatelic Traders Society (whose address is at the back of this book).

Repairs

Under this heading would come the repairs of clocks, TVs, videos, computers etc. All of these could be repaired at home provided you have the necessary skill. It may be beneficial to tie-in to appropriate hardware shops who can pass work on to you.

Toy Making

These can be wide ranging from scaled down electric powered cars to dolls or slides. Speak to your local Trading Standards Officer before you start, as toys are covered by quite a number of regulations. Consider how you will find customers – craft fairs may be one possibility.

Business Ideas – Arts & Crafts

THIS chapter encompasses a very wide range of business activities but the enterprises all tend to be of similar size (i.e. involving only one or two people) and the majority are home-based. There is also common ground in the way these businesses market and sell their products.

In terms of the total number of people who are self-employed in Britain, possibly as many as 1 in 150 are craftworkers. This means that there are at least 25,000 people working in crafts alone, half of whom are full time, in addition to artists. An interesting aspect is this is an area of economic activity where women outnumber men.

Although arts & crafts are an important non-agricultural business sector in rural communities, it is particularly important in tourist areas where income can be gained from tourists as they pass through. But one should not forget that there is a great deal of arts & crafts activity in urban areas too, where proximity to a large customer base can be an advantage.

Who become Artists & Craftspeople?

To be successful, you obviously need to be interested in arts or crafts and have a creative streak with some talent. In addition, as a self-employed person you need to have or acquire some business acumen as you will need to sell your work.

Not surprisingly, most people who become self-employed in this area have had some formal training at art college or on adult education courses, though there is still a lot to learn on the job too. Many people start in their mid-life, after a career in teaching or some other profession. About a quarter continue to teach their skill and this provides important additional income for them.

Financial Prospects

The Crafts Council report **Crafts in the 1990s** comments that "few craftspeople earn an income which equates with their extensive training, skills and working hours". The same report states that the average earnings of craftsmen (i.e. the profits from their business) was only £9,500 (in 1992) and £6,500 for craftswomen. Most full-time crafts businesses (i.e. over 60% of the total) have a turnover of less than £20,000 per year. About one third of craftworkers had goods selling from £5 upwards.

However, the survivability of this type of business is

favourable compared to other types of small business, and there is a high degree of job satisfaction.

Marketing & Sales

Many people who work in this sector complain that they have insufficient time to do both their creative work and attend to the necessary "business" side, i.e. the marketing and selling of their work, keeping their accounts up to date and chasing slow payers.

There is no simple solution to this dilemma for if you take on staff to help, you then have to earn more in order to cover their pay and you have to spend precious time training and supervising them. This is in addition to coping with the paperwork involved when you employ someone (eg PAYE, National Insurance, Sick Pay etc).

Market Research   Even before you start, as with any business, it is very important that you fully research your market as you may find that there is little commercial interest in what you plan to make or do. So just because

Business Ideas – Arts & Crafts

you were regarded at art school as having great talent, if there is little interest from potential customers, then you will soon be out of business.

Promotion   Most arts & crafts businesses produce a leaflet or brochure illustrating their work. Usually in colour, these are expensive to produce so care is needed. Thought needs to be given to ensure they don't date too quickly, so information such as prices should be printed separately (in black & white, and probably just photocopied).

Doing demonstrations, giving talks to groups of people, writing Press Releases and ensuring you are on all appropriate registers are all ways to create public awareness. If you have a workshop in part of your home, then depending on your location, you may be able to get people to come and see you at work.

Selling   If people cannot come to see you, then you need to go to see them. Attendance at exhibitions and craft fairs is one way to see people and make sales. The Chelsea Crafts Fair, the Harrogate Gift Fairs, The Spring & Autumn Fairs at the NEC and the regional fairs held at places such as Aviemore, are all important.

Getting commissions can be very important to many, but it takes time to build up and establish your reputation. Selling through shops is another avenue, but needs care and good advice.

Advice

Expert business advice is essential and this is available through Business Links (in England), local Enterprise Agencies, the Arts Council and the Crafts Council. The Crafts Council is the national body for the crafts in England, Scotland & Wales. It is an independent charity

---

THE TOP 8 CRAFTS

1. **Textiles**
2. **Ceramics**
3. **Wood**
4. **Metal/Jewellery**
5. **Glass**
6. **Toys/Musical Instruments**
7. **Graphic Crafts**
8. **Leather**

Note: Listed in terms of the numbers of craftspeople in each craft, i.e. the largest number work with Textiles.

---

funded by the Government and by its own earnings. It also produces ***Crafts*** magazine.

ADDRESS   The addresses of the Crafts Council and Arts Council are given at the end of this book ∎

Business Ideas – Direct Selling

DIRECT selling is where a manufacturer misses out the retailer entirely and sells direct to the consumer. These sales are usually made by self-employed people, who are generally home-based. The manufacturers give these salespeople various titles, such as "distributors", "consultants", "demonstrators" or "associates", sometimes prefixed by the word "independent".

Many products are sold this way, including *clothes, cosmetics, household goods, jewellery, books* and *dietary* or *nutrition products*.

The term "direct selling" covers three sales methods:

- The door-to-door approach
- Party plan selling
- Selling to contacts

Some, though not all, direct selling companies also operate a multi-level system of sales where a salesperson can recruit others and receive bonuses depending on how well their recruits perform. This way of selling is called "Network Marketing", sometimes abbreviated to "Networking", and is also known as "Multi-Level Marketing" (or MLM for short). Network Marketing is discussed later in this chapter.

Direct selling companies often continue to grow and prosper even during hard economic times when many other businesses are struggling for survival. Even through the Depression of the '30s and Recession of the '80s, many of the direct selling organisations prospered.

As a means for ordinary people to start a home-based business with minimal investment or qualifications, direct selling is important enough to merit a complete book rather than just one chapter. Direct selling is not only a growing business area but, within certain significant constraints, individuals can choose whatever level of work they want to put in (and hence the money they will earn).

In the UK, approximately £¾ billion worth of goods are sold in this way each year and involve some half a million full and part-time salespeople. The great majority of people are women working on a self-employed part-time basis, though there is usually scope to make a full-time career if you are prepared to work hard at it. Two big advantages are the complete flexibility of hours and the fact that it can be home-based.

To be interested in direct selling, you need to be self-motivated and ideally you should enjoy selling. It also helps if you are gregarious and know lots of people who can be your initial sales contacts.

There is no definition of a typical person attracted to a career in direct selling (though they must be over 18). Sales teams can range from a 20 year old typist to a 65 year old retired doctor. The money that these salespeople earn may be their sole source of income, supplementary income, or perhaps just pocket money.

Regardless of previous experience or qualifications, salespeople involved in direct selling are usually encouraged to reach the top levels of sales management which can provide outstanding financial rewards.

There was a time when some direct selling firms were accused of shady practices, so today many of the major direct selling companies belong to trade associations (see the end of this book for addresses) formed to promote high standards of trading practice and consumer protection. Members are required to comply with their association's Code of Practice.

Some Advantages Being involved with a direct selling company has many advantages over setting up a business on your own. Doing the market research, developing and testing new products, planning, pricing and sales techniques are all done by the company. All you need do is to absorb their sales training (and sometimes you have to purchase a starter pack of goods to sell). The sales procedure has been written by experts, so if you follow the training you should, in theory, make sales.

Problems People who have problems with direct selling (i.e. they don't make sufficient sales) tend to be those who: (i) don't follow the company's instructions or (ii) don't give it a try for long enough (you need to commit yourself for maybe as long as 12 months to give it a chance) or (iii) work for companies that do not have a code of ethics or (iv) become disenchanted with the endless cycle of selling and absorbing the company hype or (v) work for companies who have unsaleable goods (a not uncommon problem).

Choosing A Company Joining a company is usually quite easy. The trade associations can give you the addresses of their member companies or you may already know a distributor. It is important that you like what the company has to sell and will use the products yourself, not just sell them to others.

Once you select a company whose products you feel comfortable about selling, you will find that they are keen to get you involved. This may be because the person who recruits you will receive bonuses based on the sales that you make. This is called Network Marketing.

Network Marketing

This is also known as "Networking" or

Business Ideas – Direct Selling

Multi-Level Marketing (MLM for short). It accounts for sales of around £200 million per annum in the UK.

It works like this. You sell the products to friends and contacts. One or two of them might think they can sell it to *their* friends and so they agree to become distributors. By recruiting them, you earn bonuses that are dependent on their sales. If those new distributors recruit more people then you get a share of their sales bonuses too and so on it goes as the network expands.

The people who recruited you are called your "uplines" and the people you recruit are called your "downlines" (yes, every industry has to have its own jargon!).

Advancement in both position and profit earning need not take long. Some people who have worked hard for only six months have qualified for management training and after that have gone on to more senior levels in the company. Though it would be fair to add that progress is usually slower.

For achieving high sales levels, most direct selling companies have prizes such as holidays, jewellery, appliances, even cars. This is usually related to your recruitment success as well as your individual sales. Some people (albeit a small minority) do achieve astonishing incomes from this type of selling and the companies they work with are huge multi-billion concerns.

In theory, you can choose (virtually) whatever level of sales you feel you can cope with and wish to attain, but in reality it is rarely that simple.

An interesting aspect of network marketing is that it gives the opportunity for many people to feel real success for the first time in their lives. This not only makes them feel good but makes their colleagues feel good too.

How is Direct Selling Done?

The main ways of selling are door-to-door, party plan, and selling to contacts. Let's look briefly at each of these:

Door to Door   You will be knocking at doors not knowing what to expect and not knowing whether they will greet you and give you a chance to show your goods or whether they will be rude to you. So "cold calling" in this way can be fairly soul destroying. You also need a certain amount of nerve to keep marching up to front doors, knocking and offering a product.

In practice this type of selling tends to operate with the salesperson leaving a catalogue and then returning a few days later hoping to take an order and pick up the catalogue. Success tends to rely on repeat business. In the UK the main companies in this field report about a 25% response rate but you still need to knock on a lot of doors to make a living as you only get about 20% commission on your sales.

Party Plan   Still sometimes called "Tupperware parties" due to the company whose name is synonymous with this method of selling. Party plan has proven to be a very popular form of selling and is used as almost the only method by some companies.

The host, or more usually hostess, who is the salesperson or a friend of the salesperson, invites a group of friends and relatives to her home. The salesperson (who is sometimes called a "demonstrator") arrives with samples, or stock of the items, and demonstrates the products and then encourages the guests to place orders.

Some people who sell in this way prefer to hold stock so the customers can walk away with their goods on the

---

Tips To Help Spot Risky Schemes

1. Tend to be "get-rich-quick" schemes.

2. Tend to be companies with product(s) which are unsaleable, unattractive, over-priced or of poor quality and such that you would not use them yourself.

3. Tend to include companies where it's not clear just what you are getting until you have made an initial payment.

4. Tend to be where earnings are made primarily by recruitment of new distributors rather than by selling actual product(s).

5. Tend to be where people have to make fixed regular payments to the company.

6. Tend to be companies that have not been trading very long.

Note: Even a commercially sound and legitimate company may have one or more of the characteristics mentioned above so these tips need to be seen in context and regarded as merely an initial guide. Further research into the company concerned should reveal if their scheme is indeed sound or risky.

---

same day. Others take orders and then supply the goods later, collecting the money when they hand them over. A problem with this last method is some customers might change their minds and you then finish up with unsold goods on your hands.

Ideally, party plan selling does not require a hard sell, rather it relies on good demonstration.

Selling to Contacts   A number of companies use this approach, which is also known as "personal referral". You find the people who are interested in obtaining the product, visit them and try to make a sale. The key is to know a lot of people and be prepared to approach them all. No one is sacred! You might contact: a) your neighbours, b) friends, c) relatives, d) people who are in clubs that you belong to, such as a sports club or aerobics class, e) people in a religious group of which you are a member, f) parents of children who are studying with yours at school and (where applicable) g) contact lists that you receive from your company.

The idea is that by making contact before you visit, you know they have expressed an interest in the product, so it's not "cold calling" and you have a reasonable chance of making a sale.

But not everyone likes to be on the receiving end of this form of selling and you can become unpopular and may lose friends if you try selling to them.

FURTHER READING

There is a useful book **Multi-Level Marketing** written by Peter Clothier, published by Kogan Page and available through most bookshops.

KEY POINT

If you are being asked to sign any contract, it is highly advisable to consider getting your solicitor to look at it before you sign.

And Finally

It is probably best, at least until you get used to the methods and traps of direct selling methods, to stick with one of the companies that is a member of a trade association. But do remember that such membership is no automatic guarantee of success.

ADDRESS

The addresses of the trade associations are given at the end of this book ∎

Business Ideas – Franchising

IN franchising, you copy someone else's business with their full approval and support, under an agreement called a "franchise". In this the franchise giver (called the "franchisor") allows you to use his trade name and get his expertise with all its benefits. In exchange, you as the "franchisee" have to pay the franchisor an initial fee then on-going royalties, but the major advantages are that franchising allows you to get into business more quickly and with possibly less risk.

A Success Story   Statistics which record the failure rate of new (non-franchise) businesses vary depending upon the size of the companies considered, the number of years before trading ceases and so on, but without a doubt the figures all show a depressing picture. At least one in three of all new small businesses starting this year will not be trading in 3 year's time. Although fair comparative figures are hard to come by, it would appear that *franchised* new businesses in the UK have a better chance of surviving.

Unfortunately it is this success of franchising that has attracted many unscrupulous businesses who are offering franchises of dubious value. This chapter will therefore stress the need for caution and independent professional advice if you are thinking of taking on a franchise.

What Is Franchising?   This is when an established business is prepared to licence you to use its image, its name, its trade knowledge, its back up – in fact the whole proven business format. For any new business to be successful it

needs a number of ingredients – an adequate market for the product or service, sufficient finance, the correct stock and tools, and, very importantly, people with the right business skills (such as how to make sales). If any of these ingredients is weak or missing, the chances of failure increase dramatically, so you can see why someone setting up in business (without a franchise) has to know a lot about business and has to get most things right first time to survive and prosper.

With a franchise operation, the business you take on should be a well proven business idea and the professionals behind the franchise (called the "franchisors") should provide you (the "franchisee") with all the training and back-up you need to help you to succeed. They are keen to see you prosper because they take a percentage of your takings (called a "royalty") and so their profitability is directly linked to your profitability. This at least should ensure they will maintain their interest in what you are doing!

Who Does Franchising?   The type of franchising we are considering here is more correctly called "Business Format Franchising". Developed in the United States in the 1950s, many of the well-known franchise names are still American. In Britain, franchising is becoming more familiar to people and there are now many hundreds of companies operating franchises, including some well-known names. Around 200,000 people are employed in franchises in the UK with total sales of some £5 billion, and although the majority of these businesses are not home-based, some important ones are.

How Does Franchising Work In Practice?   Setting up any business takes money, but with a franchise operation it costs you more, because you are also paying for the business experience and proven product or service of the franchisor. In return they may set up the whole business for you, including all the legal work, the full training of yourself and finally, help you with selection of stock and/or tools. In some cases this "hand-holding" is very complete.

When you start trading there is an Operations Manual which lays down the whole format of how to run the business – it is your "bible". In good franchise operations the franchisor works in close association with you to ensure you make good profits and run a sound business. This is in his own interest too as he will want a royalty, calculated as a fixed weekly or monthly amount or a percentage (2% to 20%) of your sales. Note that this royalty is usually based on your sales figure and not on your profits! This is a subtle but important point for

---

What You Should Get In A Franchise

1. **A proven business format – that is viable.**
2. **The use of a business name and/or trade mark.**
3. **An Operations Manual.**
4. **Training in both "trade" and business skills.**
5. **An exclusive territory which is large enough.**
6. **Full support before, during and after start-up.**
7. **On-going advice and guidance.**
8. **Long-term market research to ensure the business keeps up with changes in the market place.**
9. **A contract that clearly defines the rights and obligations of both parties.**
10. **Advertising support.**
11. **Help when you get a problem.**

it means that you can still be paying a royalty to the franchisor even if you are not trading profitably (i.e. making a loss).

The rights and obligations of both parties are described in a contract which is a detailed document and forms the basis of the close association between yourself and the franchisor.

Check this document very carefully. Read all of it and ensure you understand it. Ask questions of any part you do not understand. And, before you sign it (or anything else, for that matter) it is essential you consult a solicitor. Some contracts have hostile clauses that can seriously hurt you. Remember that contract law in Scotland and England are different.

Who Should Consider Franchising? If you want to start your own business and (a) do not know what to do, (b) have a reasonable amount of capital, say £5,000 minimum and (c) are not a loner who resents anyone being involved in your venture, then becoming a franchisee is one way to get into business. Prior experience of the trade that the franchise involves is usually not a requirement as franchisors prefer to instil their own methods during the training phase. Many successful franchisees are ex-executives or ex-forces personnel, though there are franchises available to appeal to almost anyone.

Although there are certain constraints on being a franchisee such as you cannot adapt or modify the business or introduce sidelines, an important aspect of being in business for yourself, i.e. the amount of profit you can make, is mainly in your own hands.

How To Find A Suitable Franchise Many franchisors are members of the British Franchise Association (BFA). They can sell you an information pack, specifically produced for prospective franchisees, that includes a list of their members. The BFA also publishes a monthly magazine, called "Business Franchise", which is available through newsagents or by direct subscription.

In addition, Franchise Development Services publish the "Franchise Magazine" and produce an annual "UK Franchise Directory" that gives details of hundreds of franchisors. There is also the "Franchise World Directory" produced by "Franchise World" magazine.

ADDRESS

The addresses of the BFA and the franchise trade publishers are given at the end of this book.

British Franchise Association Membership Categories

Full Member
Franchisors who have a proven track record and conform to various requirements of the BFA.

Associate Member
Franchisors who conform to the BFA requirements but have not yet established a long track record.

Provisional Member
Would-be franchisors who are developing their franchise and using accredited professional advice.

Affiliate Member
These are not franchisors but organisations that are supplying services to the franchise industry (such as banks, law firms and specialist consultancies).

To meet franchisors, there are the National Franchise Exhibitions, held since 1984, and sponsored by the British Franchise Association. These are usually held twice a year, with one at Olympia in London and the other at the NEC near Birmingham. Seminars run at the same time as the exhibitions give good background information to would-be franchisees. For the adventurous, there are also franchise exhibitions held in France, Germany and the United States.

FURTHER READING

There is a useful book *Taking Up A Franchise* written by Colin Barrow and Godfrey Golzen and published by Kogan Page.

How To Assess A Franchise
When you have found several franchises which interest you, the first thing to do is to get the free franchisee information pack (it is also called a prospectus) from each franchisor in question. Study the information carefully. It should describe the franchise in detail, give the business background of the key executives, the training to be given, the initial investment required (with a break-down) and give financial performance

Business Ideas – Franchising

figures (actual, not just projections). The prospectus should also give details as to how long the agreement would be for, the renewal conditions and what happens if either party wants to terminate the agreement.

If your bank has a franchise unit, arrange an appointment to see them and get their advice. If your bank does not have such a unit, you might consider visiting a bank that does, though naturally they will hope that you will use their bank should you start in business.

The next step is to make an appointment to visit the franchisor's head office, however far away it might be. During the interview, you need to ask probing questions and write down their answers. Questions to ask, include:

1. *When was the business established?*
2. *Are they members of the BFA? And if not, why?*
3. *How many outlets are there in the UK?*
4. *How many outlets have ceased trading, and why?*
5. *Who are the people behind the franchise?*
6. *How good is the company's financial performance?*
7. *What is the initial capital required?*
8. *What are the addresses of franchisees you can visit.*
9. *What is the annual royalty charge?*
10. *What do you get for your money?*
11. *What on-going support do they give?*
12. *Are there other charges, eg advertising?*
13. *What are the long-term prospects for the franchise?*
14. *What is the length of the Agreement?*
15. *Who is the competition?*

If satisfied so far, this is also the time to ask to see a specimen contract which you need to take away to read carefully and show to your solicitor. After the meeting, visit at least two of their franchisees (of your own choice) and get their viewpoint.

Up to now you have had to rely on the franchisor's view of their product or service and the market place. It is now time for you to do your own market research. You need to find out just how strong the market demand is for such products or services, what customers think of the franchise and how strong is the competition.

KEY POINT

Before you make any commitment to a franchise, ensure you see both an accountant and a solicitor.

While you are busy assessing a particular franchise, the franchisor will be taking a very close look at you. Rather like a job interview, a good franchisor will be keen to ensure you are suitable for the task ahead.

Raising The Finance A common complaint is that franchisors understate the necessary capital to start the business and entirely omit the living costs you will need to survive domestically until the business begins to make a profit (which can take many months, even for a good business). Other ways a franchisor can make the start-up figure seem less than actual is by quoting a low figure to purchase a second-hand van or other piece of essential equipment. VAT is also often omitted (which you will have to pay but not be able to recover unless you are going to be VAT-registered yourself). The figures also often omit your own legal and accountancy fees.

Business Ideas – Franchising

You may have capital through savings, inheritance or redundancy but you could still need some additional finance to launch your venture. With one of the better known franchises, the banks are sometimes happy to fund up to two-thirds of the start-up costs, due to the proven record of these businesses. In contrast, banks are usually reluctant to fund more than half the costs of a non-franchised venture.

Several of the main High Street banks have specialist franchise units and their advice should be sought if you are considering franchising. The banks have access to confidential data which could either encourage or discourage you from proceeding with your plans.

Some Of The Small Print   One misconception surrounds the idea of "exclusive" territories. The franchise you take on may indeed give you an exclusive territory *for that franchise* but that does not prevent a rival company (franchised or not) from trading in your area. In fact, many franchise businesses have rival franchises to cope with in addition to non-franchised competitors.

Another question you need to ask is what happens if you are really unhappy with your franchise after you have started trading. You will by that time have signed an irrevocable contract with probably no easy out clause. Usually you will have to find a buyer for your franchise but any would-be buyer needs to be approved by the franchisor and it may be difficult finding a buyer if your business is not trading successfully. A franchise agreement is a binding contract. Once you sign it, you are bound for its term (usually from 5 to 10 years)!

Cautions:
Taking on a franchise does not guarantee success as *some have failed* whilst others fail to meet projected turn-over figures. A franchisor's membership of the British Franchise Association in itself does not lessen the need for careful checking on your part.

Even if you join a good, well-managed, ethical franchise, your own business could still have problems due to local competition and trading circumstances.

Franchising works for many thousands of people and can work for you too, but the message is quite clear – choose your franchise very carefully indeed.

Even if successful, the business will require much hard work and time for it to become established. Franchising is definitely not for the faint-hearted ■

Home-based Franchises

Below we list just some of the franchise opportunities that you may be able to run from your home:

Book-keeping Services	**Home Delivery (eg soft drinks, frozen food)**
Business Transfer Agents	**Interior Decoration Consultants**
Car Driving Instruction	**Kitchen Cupboard Renovation**
Car Tuning (mobile)	**Security Equipment Sales**
Cleaning (domestic, offices, carpets etc)	**Specialised Employment Agencies**
Computerised Debt Collection Services	**Telesales**
Dress Hire	**Training**
Educational Toys & Games	**Van-based Delivery To Auto Trade**
Financial Services	**Will Writing**
Health & Beauty	

For more information on these business ideas, contact the appropriate franchises.

Business Ideas – Teaching

IT was George Bernard Shaw who said that those who can, do, and those who can't, teach. Perhaps Shaw should have added that those who have done it, can teach others.

If you have a skill, then with some effort and minimal investment, you can make it pay by passing on your knowledge and experience to others. Home workshops and classes can be fun and relaxing and a profitable experience for both the person teaching and the person learning.

What To Teach?

Do you have some qualification or skill? Are you particularly knowledgeable about some hobby or craft? You may have spent your years looking after a home – cleaning, cooking, baking, polishing, gardening, making things for the family. When you think about it, there are a lot of skills used in the home which others would gladly learn from you, eg how to prepare cheap and quick meals, how to save money on clothes, how to grow better vegetables and flowers; how to sew etc.

If you can do it, teach it!

The first rule of success is to find a need and fill it. A good starting point is to check with your local adult education classes. Have a look at their course lists and see what they offer. Make a phone call and try to find out which classes are popular and which ones are not and why. Then consider your own abilities and interests and try to match them up. Look for trends, check in the newspapers, have a look around. Can you develop a course that is even more attractive than those on offer at the local college?

Once you have decided on a skill, subject or course you would like to teach, you will need to do some market research to check its likely viability. Mention it to everyone you know to see their reaction. Listen to the feedback. You could start a class with just your friends as this has several advantages. First of all, it gives you confidence. If you make a few mistakes, they will be forgiving. It will also give you experience in handling a class and guidelines as to how much to fit into each session. Your friends can tell what they found interesting or boring to help you adjust your course.

It is best to have a speciality and stick to it. As one Italian cookery class teacher puts it "I don't teach Chinese cooking and I wouldn't expect a Chinese cook to be teaching pasta dishes either. Do what you do best and eventually people will come looking for you".

The Where? the When? and the How?

Most subjects can be taught in an urban or rural location, but a nice country setting can be an additional attraction particularly with residential courses. Craft courses are often held in the workshops of a craft business which has the appropriate facilities and planning permission.

Courses can be an hour or so per week, an evening each week, a week-end or even longer. Not surprisingly, residential courses tend to be held over a week-end or for a full week. Some people who run these courses from large houses, offer accommodation themselves (though they would need to consider the implications of Planning Permission, Fire Certificates etc etc), while others simply put students up in a local hotel.

Although teaching can be done on a one-to-one basis, this is not as cost effective – you can make more per hour teaching a group, and the student misses out on the interaction with other students. However, some teaching (music lessons and tutoring are good examples) are usually done one-to-one.

You need to be clear in your mind why someone will want to attend your classes. Is it just to have fun while learning a new skill, to gain a qualification or perhaps to learn some skill that they can use to earn an income?

Perhaps your students want to learn some skill that they can use to earn an income?

You may need to run several courses to suit different skill levels of students.

If you are not running a full day or week-end course, then look at the possibility of teaching some classes in the day time and some in the evening. For instance if you are giving cookery classes, there are a lot of working men and women who could not come to a daytime class. Equally some people could not come to an evening class due to family commitments.

 Contact your local authority to see if you need planning permission (or other approvals) and speak to your solicitor and insurers too.

KEY POINT

Finding Customers

You should keep two points in mind: advertise to attract students and continually research your market. Work out who is going to come to your classes, and why. Once you have held a few classes, new students will find you as your reputation spreads. Local newspapers (or other publications, as appropriate) may be interested in doing articles on you and this will lead to more contacts. This editorial coverage is about the best "advertising" you can get as people may not look at your advertisement in a publication but they will usually read the articles.

If your likely students are coming from far afield then an article in a local newspaper will not help much and you will need to advertise and get articles in appropriate newspapers or specialist magazines that these people are likely to read. Such adverts can be expensive, so need careful thought.

If your customers are mainly local, you could ask your local library to see if they would be interested in you setting up a lecture or giving a demonstration.

Whenever you do give lectures or demonstrations, have a supply of business cards or brochures ready to hand out as it is the perfect time to sign up new students. But you still want to attract the ones that walk away unsure, so give them a brochure with an enrolment slip.

As you are setting yourself up as an expert, it helps your credibility if you have a qualification or perhaps have written magazine articles or books on the subject.

Calculating What To Charge

If you are running a course for a group of people, then to calculate what you need to charge each student, you first need to know exactly how much it costs you to run the course.

---

8 TIPS FOR RUNNING A GOOD CLASS

1. Choose a good setting in pleasant surroundings for your class. It must be warm and have comfortable seating. There may be an opportunity to display things of relevance to stimulate the class.

2. At the first session ask your students why they are interested in your class, assess their present knowledge levels and find out what they expect to learn. That may lead you to adjust the lesson plans that you have prepared. (It will also give you a guide to other possibilities for courses you could run).

3. Be fully prepared. Take the time to organise your lessons so that your class is conducted in a logical sequence and the students can have the chance to get the maximum benefit from what you are saying. You may want to prepare for them summaries of the points that you are making, so that they can enlarge on those as they go through the session.

4. Keep your explanations simple. Remember that you might know your subject matter backwards but the students need to understand the basics first. Develop the theme from simple steps to begin with, moving to more complex steps later on.

5. Vary your lesson approach. Do not lecture for too long, instead you could show slides and videos, take a field trip or do demonstrations. You could also break the class into little groups, where they can discuss things and then come and report to the whole class.

6. Be flexible. If you are too school-oriented as far as your approach to the classes are concerned, you will find that a lot of your clients will lose interest very quickly. Don't talk down to your students.

7. Involve your students fully, by (i) raising points that are relevant to individuals and (ii) getting them to ask questions and generally to participate fully in the discussions. This may require you to gently encourage shy members of the class. Try also to make the most of the experiences of class members themselves and avoid talking for too long yourself.

8. Courses should be not only informative but also FUN!

Business Ideas – Teaching

So you need to add up the costs of:

(1) Your advertisements (and other promotions);
(2) Brochures (and the cost of mailing them out);
(3) Correspondence and phone calls with applicants;
(4) Course notes & other materials you hand out or use;
(5) Meals and accommodation (if applicable);
(6) Any other costs that you can think of, eg extra heating.

You then need to work out how many people you can cope with (and how many are likely to apply). You divide your costs by this number to find your base cost/student. Next you want to add your profit, but first you need to have an idea as to (a) what your competitors charge and (b) how much your students are prepared to pay.

Then with all that information, work out your figure, double check the arithmetic and ensure you are charging as much as you think you can (as nobody will thank you for making it cheap and you will almost certainly have under-estimated your true outgoings). If you work out a few figures you should be able to strike some sort of happy medium between making a reasonable profit and frightening people off by the cost of the classes.

One-to-One Tuition   If you are giving one-to-one tuition (such as music lessons or tutoring) the calculations are done differently. Such tuition is usually charged on an *hourly basis* and is very much dictated by what other people are charging i.e. the "going rate" locally. But what you can do is to add up your outgoings as before, then deduct that from your hourly rate to see what you are actually making per hour.

If your students tend not to last for a whole course, then you could consider offering a discount for paying for the whole course in advance.

Additional Revenue   Useful extra cash can be earned by selling materials and books to students, but never at a price higher than they could buy them elsewhere, so you would need to purchase them wholesale to make a profit.

Future Courses   Finally, if possible, structure your course so that at the end your students will be encouraged to take another course with you at some time in the future. This new course could be a follow-on, or a related subject, or you could grade your courses for "beginners", "intermediate standard", "advanced level" and "expert", thereby giving students a logical progression to follow. By doing this you hope that they will start as beginners and, in time, work their way up through the higher level courses.

General   Whatever you plan to teach, be sure your home insurance fully covers you (including claims from students) and that you are not in breach of planning regulations or other legalities – you could check with your local Council. As always, take professional advice before you start, however modest a scale you propose to run your business.

COURSE IDEAS . . . . .

Just some examples of the courses which could be given from home include (in alphabetical order):

Cookery   This is always a popular subject and very diverse. Cordon Bleu, Cordon Vert, microwave cooking, "quick dishes for dads", the many national cuisines etc. You can demonstrate or (if your facilities permit this) allow individuals to make each dish themselves. It can be fun to eat the food at the end of the lesson. It is useful to hand out a typed recipe for whatever has been cooked during the class so that they can try it again at home. Check with your local Environmental Health Officer as to what Food Hygiene Regulations might apply.

Crafts   This covers a wide range of possibilities. If you have a definite artistic skill and would like to teach others, then this would certainly be an option to consider. You would, of course, need to be able to offer the appropriate facilities for your students.

Curtains & Pelmet Making   This type of course usually covers more than basic curtain making as it can include all aspects of soft furnishings and colour co-ordination in a room.

Flower Arranging   Another favourite course. It has a seasonal aspect due to the availability of cut flowers.

Furniture Making   This usually involves the students making a specific item during the course, be it a stool or something a little more ambitious, depending on their skill. This course obviously requires the use of suitable workshop facilities.

Furniture Restoration (& Upholstery)   This can involve repairing, painting, french polishing and caning. Again it requires suitable facilities.

Business Ideas – Teaching

Health & Beauty   These are classes in which you will teach women about make-up, hair, skin care and choice of clothing. Although you may give the course over many weeks, you could charge a fee per session but it may be better to encourage them to attend by signing them up for the complete course and getting them to pay in one go at the beginning.

If discussing diet, be careful about the legal implications of endorsing any product and suggest that anyone who is going to use any proprietary diet first sees their doctor. This advice also holds if they plan to change the way they exercise. This is to cover yourself for any legal responsibility you have if something goes wrong when they do these things. You might be able to arrange exercise sessions in conjunction with someone else who has expertise in that particular area.

Interior Design   Some Interior Design courses are to give students the skills to set up their own interior design businesses.

Machine Knitting   Machine knitting is a very popular pastime and a money earner too (see the entry under "Knitting" in the earlier chapter **Business Ideas – A-Z**). If you are good at this, there is scope to teach others.

Music Lessons   Music lessons are very popular in all parts of the country and they are very easy to set up, provided you have the appropriate musical skills. To get students, you could try advertising in your local newspapers and talk to everyone you know about your idea. Speak to the music teachers in your local schools, but remember that many of them also give private music lessons after school. You could also try speaking to your local musical instrument shops. Finally, if you are having children or adults coming to your house then you need to check out your insurance cover.

Painting   There are courses in watercolours, oils and drawing. There is also interest in more specialised painting techniques such as marbling, stencilling and painted furniture. If you are an accomplished artist then this is certainly an option to consider.

Photography   Each year we spend around half a billion pounds on films and processing. Our obsession with capturing images on film is also reflected by the number of camera shops and the interest in photography magazines. Although many people are happy just to take holiday snaps, others are interested in achieving more with their photo gear.

The use of video cameras has opened up a whole new area and judging from some of the truly dreadful amateur videos that one has to endure, there is certainly scope for users to learn the correct way to use such equipment.

Sewing   A sewing course might be a bit hard to set up and certainly more costly to run unless you have students who will bring their own sewing machines to each session. Otherwise you have to provide the machines for them. Try to find simple patterns which lead to useful articles. Nobody wants to just sew samples, people want to make things which they find attractive or useful. However, you do not have to finish a garment every session. Your students can do some of it at home but you should try to have them complete an article every two or three weeks otherwise they can become bored with it and will stop attending.

You could consider selling profitable sidelines such as buttons and patterns, maybe even sewing machines. If you have the skill, you can also extend your classes to cover pattern making and designing.

Tutoring   Tutoring high school, college or university students is probably one of the easier types of course to run, provided you are a teacher or lecturer or have appropriate academic training. The schools or colleges in your area should be able to tell you what others are charging.

Writing   Accomplished authors are sometimes prepared to coach others and give their students hints to help them to have their own work published.

Some other ideas for subjects you could teach: astrology, bonsai, embroidery, English for non-English speakers, foreign languages, gardening and herb growing ∎

Business Ideas – Writing

THERE are many people who would like to write for a living or at least see their writing being published and to make something out of it financially. Unfortunately nothing is as simple as it looks. Writing may be fun but there are many problems that people run into when they decide they are going to write professionally.

You could write novels, non-fiction books, poetry or short stories. Alternatively you could write articles for magazines or newspapers. But before we look at these, let us consider some of the basics that will apply no matter what kind of writing you are going to do.

Equipment These days nearly everyone who is going to write professionally uses a word processor. You can either use a dedicated word processor or a computer with word processing software.

Many publishers now insist that work is supplied to them on computer disk. The advantage to them is significant as it means the text doesn't have to be retyped again when typesetting.

If you cannot type, you seriously need to consider learning to type first before you embark on any professional writing.

Presentation Presentation is where many hopeful writers fall down. A neat and tidy manuscript means just about everything. It is probably psychological but the more expensive the paper, the blacker the print and the cleaner the type, the easier it is to read and the more likely it will be accepted by the person reading it.

Magazines, newspapers and book publishers frequently express their disgust at the quality of the manuscripts that come in . . . . they arrive pinned together in the corner; typed on odd bits of paper on an old machine so that you can hardly read the print; covered in coffee stains and dry blobs of correction fluid; they have dog-eared corners and half-flattened creases (showing that other editors have already thumbed through and rejected them).

There is nothing that shows up the amateur writer more than when they type their manuscripts using single spacing and without sufficient margins all around. The double spacing and wide margins are necessary for an editor to scribble comments. You should type on only one side of the paper and don't fasten the paper together with anything more permanent than a paper clip. Number the pages, in the top right corner, in case they fall apart.

If your piece or article is a substantial length, preface it with a title page which should give the title, your name and address, a daytime contact phone number and an estimate of the number of words. You should keep photocopies of everything you send out.

Any manuscript that is more than five or six pages long should be kept flat and sent, unfolded, in a suitably sized A4 envelope. Mark your name and address clearly on the back of the envelope. Unless the article has been commissioned, always include a stamped addressed envelope.

Keep records and receipts of your expenditure because all your expenses, materials, typing costs, photocopying, postage and the host of other outgoings can usually be set against your income tax liability provided you are self-employed and you earn income from your writing activity.

Pseudonyms It is handy to have another name or *nom de plume* that you can use if needed. You may want to write regularly for one publication under one name and another publication under another. Novelists who also write practical non-fiction articles sometimes do so under a different name and vice versa. Another occasion when you may wish to use a pseudonym is where your name does not fit the image of the market. For instance, you may be a man writing a romance story for a woman's magazine. In that case a female name is probably essential.

Business Cards You should get some business cards printed and they should be well designed. Try to do something that is a little different and ensure the word "writer" appears on the business cards. If you can write on some specialist subject, then state that on your cards too.

Portfolio As soon as you start getting your work in print, you should begin to compile a cuttings book or portfolio that you can show to future publishers. You could use one of the Rexel display books which have clear A3 or A4 size pockets into which you can slip your cuttings. Put your recent work at the front. You should preface each article with a cover of the issue in which it appears.

Put some thought into how best to display the variety of your writing. It might be better to have several thin portfolios rather than one thick one, depending on the topics or areas that you have worked in. A loose-leaf portfolio is essential so that you have the freedom to reorganise it, to update it and to tailor your type of presentation to the kinds of people you are approaching. For instance, if what you want to do is to interview people, and you are then trying to sell articles based on those interviews, then fill the folder with just those articles.

Vanity Publishing Sometimes in the small ads in newspapers or magazines you will find something along the lines of *"If you have written a book that deserves to be published, then write to us. Your book may be published and marketed."* When you contact these companies you find that they want you to pay them to publish your book. In the trade this is called "vanity publishing" and it is really not a commercial proposition for you (i.e. you are unlikely to make any money doing this). It is only relevant if you are determined to see your work in print and are happy to pay several thousand pounds for that.

If you have written a good book, somewhere there is a publisher who will pay you to have it published. If you have to pay to have it published then it probably means that your book is not good enough. That is the horrible truth of it.

SOME LEGALITIES

Copyright Copyright exists as soon as a work is created in material form. There is no formal method of registration in the UK and it expires only well after the author has died. Copyright is intended to prevent the unauthorised copying of work, be it literary, dramatic, musical or artistic. Copyright does not protect an idea, as such, but it may cover the description of the idea.

Plagiarism Plagiarism is literary theft and occurs if you copy other people's work and pretend it is your own. Obviously, you should not set out to deliberately copy work that someone else has produced because you will find yourself not only in breach of copyright but also discredited as a writer.

Libel A libel is a statement which defames the good reputation of a person.

If you do libel someone it could cost you a great deal of money, so you must be very careful to avoid writing material that could lead to an action for libel. You do not even have to mention the specific name of the person, if that person is identifiable in the context of what you write. In most cases the publisher will edit out anything defamatory anyway because they may be sued too.

Contracts It is vital you have a written contract or agreement with the publisher. This might just be a letter covering all the points.

FURTHER READING The book trade's standard reference book on contracts is **Publishing Agreements**, edited by Charles Clark.

Payment Sometimes it seems that payment is a delicate, almost embarrassing problem to be mentioned as little as possible. In just about every other business the purchaser asks how much they are going to have to pay. For some reason, freelance writers often seem reluctant to mention the subject of fees early in the negotiations.

FURTHER READING A good guide to fees and royalties is the National Union of Journalist's **Guide to Freelancing**, available from the NUJ (address at the end of this book).

The guide is relevant to any writer, not just NUJ members.

PROBLEMS THAT WRITERS SUFFER

1. People's failure to recognise it's a job
They see you at home apparently not doing very much. You may be doing some very creative work but people will still interrupt.

Writing is a very solitary activity. You need to be very determined and able to reject any activity that takes you away from your work. People often misunderstand the situation and think you are simply anti-social.

2. Rejection In freelance writing everyone has to learn to face rejection. Some rejection slips are very well composed, others are just downright rude. When you first start out the disappointment of getting a rejection slip can be very intense. Well, take heart, it gets easier as you go along and when you have enough to wallpaper a room it becomes very easy indeed. The only remedy is to keep going. There is a terrible temptation to give up when you get your first rejection slip.

What you should do is to take another look at the publisher's output, i.e. their magazine, newspaper or other books, as appropriate to yourself. Does your style, tone and story line fit with the publisher's?

3. Acceptance This does not sound like much of a problem but there are two reactions you have to be very careful of. First, assuming it is just a piece of luck, like winning the lottery. It is not luck, it is a professional achievement. Second, assuming that all your worries are over. One acceptance does not make a summer – and is very unlikely to make you rich and famous.

4. Writer's block This can be a real problem! It is experienced by just about all writers but it affects different people in different ways. Some writers who are brilliantly fluent, suddenly find themselves with nothing to say. When professionals are caught like that, they

Business Ideas – Writing

"Sorry Mr H, I got 'cleaners block', so I thought I'd just write me memoirs"

sometimes turn to more mundane tasks like tidying up their office or catching up with paperwork.

THE DIFFERENT MEDIA

BOOKS

Each year there are about 80,000 new books published in Britain. This is in addition to the huge number of existing titles and reprints that are already on sale. Although this massive figure covers all types of books (novels, non-fiction, academic, textbooks etc), the supply of books exceeds likely demand by some considerable factor, resulting in many books being loss makers for their publishers. It is against that difficult commercial background that the new, untried, author tries his or her luck.

A writer will get a royalty of between 7½% (on mass-market paperbacks) up to 15% for a good selling hardback. 10% is not uncommon, so if a book retails for £9.95, the royalty would be almost £1, but as the print run is often in the low thousands, the total return on many months of hard work can be disappointing. The hope is always that the initial print run will sell out and the book is reprinted. If this process is repeated then it should produce a reasonable royalty income in the long term.

Writing Novels This is probably one of the hardest areas to get into. Each day publishers receive large piles of manuscripts (mostly rubbish) and therefore some editors don't even take the trouble to send out rejection slips. The problem facing any publisher with an unknown author is that the public wants to read books written by known authors and trying to launch an unknown author with their first novel is not only hard work but an expensive gamble too. A literary first novel usually achieves well under 1,000 sales in hardback. These days, with a few exceptions, even so-called "best-sellers" may only sell a few thousand copies in hardback. To get that all important first novel published is a high hurdle to cross and only a very good manuscript has any chance at all.

Writing Non-Fiction Most writers of non-fiction hold down a full-time job in industry or as academics. They can therefore afford to spend time writing a book that may not be published or will only generate a pittance (but adds to their credentials). Academics are particularly lucky as they can recommend their own books to their students, thereby generating extra sales.

Writing Poetry It often seems that there are more people writing poetry than actually buying poetry books or reading poetry. It is therefore very difficult to get a book of poems published. If you are interested in writing poetry as a form of income, you should know that there are not more than a dozen English-speaking poets who make a good living out of their writing. Before you have any chance to get your poems published in book form you would usually need to have had poems published in magazines. Poetry publishing is very specialised.

Finding A Book Publisher

There are two possible approaches:

1. Write the whole book and then try to find a publisher for it. This means hawking the manuscript around from publisher to publisher.

2. Write just an outline as a synopsis including the main event that occurs in

the book, then write one or two chapters, and send it to a publisher asking whether they would be interested in such a book. In that way you can save yourself a tremendous amount of time.

There are thousands of different publishers and most specialise in certain well defined areas. In other words, if they receive an unsolicited manuscript on a subject that is outwith their specialisation they will *not* publish it, however good it might be. Many people who are new to writing books make the basic mistake of approaching the wrong publishers with their manuscript.

Once you have a manuscript to offer you need to take the time and effort to produce a short-list of likely publishers. You create this list by looking in book shops and libraries to find books similar to your own and then you look inside to see who published them. (Note: it is the name of the "publisher" you need, not the "printer").

FURTHER READING Consult the annual **Writers' & Artist' Yearbook** which not only lists all the main British publishers but also includes many articles of relevance to new writers. Essential reading!

In any event, do not expect publishers to comment on why your manuscript is unsuitable – it is not their job to teach people how to write!

MAGAZINES & NEWSPAPERS

Writing for Magazines Have a look at the business idea "Magazine Publishing" in the chapter **Business Ideas – A-Z**. This will give you a quick background to the magazine world. One of the good things about writing for magazines is that you get paid reasonably quickly. Freelance journalists can have fairly regular sources of income, unlike book writers who might have to wait several years before there are any returns. On the other hand, journalism is usually very competitive and so your work has to be better than average before you have any chance of acceptance.

If you are planning to write articles for magazines you should take the trouble to learn a bit about how magazines are financed and how they are put together. You need to realise that there is a major emphasis on selling as much advertising space as possible.

Submitting Material Realistically you are unlikely to break into the big league consumer magazine world as an unknown freelance writer. You have much more chance of getting something published in a specialist consumer magazine or trade magazine. The usual advice is that you should first send a letter to the editor of the magazine you have targeted. The letter should explain your *expertise* and give the editor a list of articles you could write – a heading and a few sentences to describe each article.

If you are asked to submit an article, do remember to find out what length is required (usually given in terms of a word count), what illustrations there will be, the deadline, payment, and how the magazine wants the article submitted – on computer disk is becoming the norm these days.

Writing Short Stories Unlike writers of full-length books who may be able to get away with submitting a short synopsis, as a short story writer you will have to complete the story before you can interest anyone. Before going any further it needs to be pointed out that getting short stories published is very difficult (i.e. it is almost impossible as an unknown writer). Whereas the advice given to writers of articles is to first submit a letter, as a writer of short stories you really need to let the editor see what you can do. So you need to send your manuscript but do enclose a stamped addressed envelope and in your covering letter ask for the manuscript back if they don't intend to use it.

Writing for Newspapers Newspapers are generally even harder to get into than magazines and you normally have to be a member of the NUJ and had journalistic training and experience.

Deadlines With any publication, deadlines are critical. If an editor says your article must arrive by a certain date, then you must meet that date ■

Business Ideas – INDEX

Business Ideas – INDEX

Useful Addresses

Note: Addresses are listed alphabetically by chapter.

Chapter: Getting Started in Your Business

Business Connect (in Wales) – for your nearest, contact the Welsh Development Agency, tel: 0345 775577.

Business Information Source (in the Highlands & Islands)
– for your nearest office, contact Highlands & Islands Enterprise, tel: 01463 234171.

Business Links (in England) – for your nearest, look in Yellow Pages, under "Business enterprise agencies".

Business Shops (in Scotland, excluding Highlands & Islands)
– for your nearest, contact Scottish Enterprise, tel: 0141-248 2700 or tel: 0800 787878.

Prince's Scottish Youth Business Trust (Glasgow), tel: 0141-248 4999 or 0800 842842.

Prince's Youth Business Trust, 18 Park Square East, London NW1 4LH. Tel: 0171-543 1234 or 0800 842842.

Shell Livewire, Hawthorn House, Forth Banks, Newcastle-upon-Tyne NE1 3SG. Tel: 0191-261 5584 or tel: 0345 573252
– Web site: http://www.shell-livewire.org

Chapter: Making it Legal

Addresses of Companies House:

In England and Wales: Companies House, Crown Way, Maindy, Cardiff CF4 3UZ. Tel: 01222 380801.
or: Companies House, 55-71 City Rd, London EC1Y 1BB. Tel: 0171-253 9393.

In Scotland: Companies House, 37 Castle Terrace, Edinburgh EH1 2EB. Tel: 0131-535 5800.

In Northern Ireland: Companies Registry, IDB House, 64 Chichester St, Belfast BT1 4JX. Tel: 01232 234488.

(There are also Satellite Offices in Leeds, Birmingham, Glasgow and Manchester).

Chapter: Business Ideas A-Z

ACCOUNTS BOOK-KEEPING
The Association of Chartered Certified Accountants, 1 Woodside Place, Glasgow G3 7QF. Tel: 0141-331 1046.
(Note: Formerly known as The Chartered Association of Certified Accountants).

BEAUTICIAN
The International Health & Beauty Council, 46 Aldwick Rd, Bognor Regis, W. Sussex PO21 2PN. Tel: 01243 842064.

BURGLAR ALARM INSTALLING
IFSEC Trade show – the organisers are Miller Freeman, tel: 0181-742 2828.
SITO (Security Industry Training Organisation), Security House, Barbourne Rd, Worcester WR1 1RS. Tel: 01905 20004.

Chapter: Business Ideas A-Z (continued)

BUSINESS CONSULTANT

Institute of Management Consultancy, 5th Floor, 32-33 Hatton Garden, London EC1N 8DL. Tel: 0171-242 2140.
(Note: Formerly known as the Institute of Management Consultants).

CHILD MINDING

National Child Minding Association, 8 Masons Hill, Bromley, Kent BR2 9EY. Tel: 0181-464 6164.

DISK JOCKEY

The Performing Right Society Ltd, 29-33 Berners St, London W1P 4AA. Tel: 0171-580 5544.
Phonographic Performance Ltd, 1 Upper James St, London W1R 3HG. Tel: 0171-437 0311.

DRIVING INSTRUCTOR

British School of Motoring Ltd, 81-87 Hartfield Rd, Wimbledon, London SW19 3TJ. Tel: 0181-540 8262.
Driving Standards Agency, Stanley House, 56 Talbot St, Nottingham NG1 5GU. Tel: 0115 9012500.

EXPORTING

DTI's Export Credits Guarantee Department, 2 Exchange Tower, Harbour Exchange Sq, London E14 9GS. Tel: 0171-512 7000.

FREELANCING

National Union of Journalists, Acorn House, 314 Gray's Inn Rd, London WC1X 8DP. Tel: 0171-278 7916.

INVENTING

The Patent Office, Concept House, Cardiff Rd, Newport, Gwent NP9 1RH. Tel: 0645 500 505.

MANUFACTURER'S AGENT

British Agents Register, 24 Mount Parade, Harrogate, Yorkshire HG1 1BP. Tel: 01423 560608.
Manufacturer's Agents' Association, 1 Somers Rd, Reigate, Surrey RH2 9DU. Tel: 01737 241025.

SECOND-HAND CAR SALES

British Car Auctions Ltd (Head Office), Expedier House, Portsmouth Rd, Hindhead, Surrey GU26 6TJ. Tel: 01428 607440.
(Note: Formerly known as ADT Auctions Ltd).
Equifax plc, tel: 01722 422422.   (Note: Formerly known as HPI Equifax).

SOFTWARE WRITING

Atlantic Coast plc, The Shareware Village, Colyton, Devon EX13 6HA. Tel: 01297 552222.
(Note: Formerly known as The Software Source).
The Public Domain & Shareware Library, PO Box 131, Crowborough, Sussex TN6 1WS. Tel: 01892 663298.

SOME OTHER BUSINESS IDEAS:

Employment Agency Standards Office, DTI, 1D5, 1 Victoria St, London SW1H 0ET. Tel: 0645 555105.
(Note: Formerly known as the Employment Agencies Licensing Office).
Philatelic Traders Society, 107 Charterhouse St, London EC1M 6PT. Tel: 0171-490 1005.

Useful Addresses

Chapter: Arts & Crafts

Crafts Council, 44a Pentonville Rd, Islington, London N1 9BY. Tel: 0171-278 7700.
Arts Council of England, 14 Gt Peter St, London SW1P 3NQ. Tel: 0171-333 0100.
Scottish Arts Council, 12 Manor Pl, Edinburgh EH3 7DD. Tel: 0131-226 6051.

Chapter: Direct Selling

Direct Marketing Association UK Ltd, Haymarket House, 1 Oxendon St, London SW1Y 4EE. Tel: 0171-321 2525.
Direct Selling Association, 29 Floral St, London WC2E 9DP. Tel: 0171-497 1234.

Chapter: Franchising

British Franchise Association, Thames View, Newtown Rd, Henley-on-Thames RG9 1HG. Tel: 01491 578049.
Franchise Development Services Ltd publish "The Franchise Magazine" and the annual "UK Franchise Directory".
    Address: Franchise House, 56 Surrey St, Norwich NR1 3FD. Tel: 01603 620301.
Franchise World publish "Franchise World" magazine and the annual "Franchise World Directory".
    Address: James House, 37 Nottingham Rd, London SW17 7EA. Tel: 0181-767 1371.

Chapter: Writing

National Union of Journalists, Acorn House, 314 Gray's Inn Rd, London WC1X 8DP. Tel: 0171-278 7916.

Tax Data Page

Note 1: The figures and rates of tax quoted on this page are those for the 1998/99 tax year.
Note 2: To have correct and up-to-date information, please check with the relevant tax authorities.

INCOME TAX

Lower Rate: 20% (for that portion of taxable income below £4,300)
Basic Rate: 23%
Higher Rate: 40% (for that portion of taxable income exceeding £27,100)

Personal Allowances:
Single Person: £4,195
Married Couple or Additional Personal Allowance: £1,900 (but relief is restricted to 15%)

PAYE: There is a lower limit, ie unless an employee's Tax Code is to the contrary, there is normally no Income Tax to be deducted if an employee's wage is less than the PAYE threshold.

Simple Tax Accounts: For Sole Traders or Partnerships, if your annual turnover is below £15,000, then in the appropriate part of the SELF ASSESSMENT Tax Return, instead of providing a detailed breakdown of your income and expenses, you simply fill in: (1) your turnover, (2) allowable business expenses and (3) your net profits.

NATIONAL INSURANCE

Class 1 (Employees/Directors)   Lower Limit: £64 weekly or £278 monthly, ie there is normally no National Insurance contribution (or Employers contribution) on earnings below this limit.

Class 1A (Cars and Fuel)   This is a contribution (only by Employers) if cars are made available for private use to their Employees or Directors.

Class 2 (Sole Traders/Partners)   £6.35 per week. (The Small Earnings Exception limit is £3,590 per annum).

Class 4 (Sole Traders/Partners)   Calculated as 6% of profits between £7,310 and £25,220, ie no Class 4 is due if taxable profits are under £7,310.

CORPORATION TAX
The tax rate for small companies is 21% for profits up to £300,000

VALUE ADDED TAX (VAT)
Standard Rate = 17.5%. Registration threshold = £50,000 (turnover)

CAPITAL GAINS TAX (CGT)
Annual exemption = first £6,800 of chargeable gain.

INDEX
(Excluding Business Ideas – see page 112)

Great Books For Small Business . . .

The Greatest Sales & Marketing Book (3rd edn)
The Practical Action Guide for a Small Business

Full of ideas to increase your sales. How to advertise successfully. Many worked examples, eg Pricing, a Press Release, a leaflet. Tips to survive a Recession. Advice to keep down overheads. Research – how to do it and how it helps. Excellent reviews in, for example, *The Times, Money Week* and *British Business* magazine. Updated regularly. 120 pages and highly illustrated.

By **Peter Hingston**   ISBN 0 906555 17 5   **£7.50**

SOLD OUT

The Greatest Little Business Book (8th edn)
The Essential Guide to Starting a Small Business

A comprehensive reference book and an international best-seller, recommended by small business advisers. Many worked examples, eg a Cashflow, Business Plan and Partnership Agreement. Also: legalities, raising finance, finding premises, employing staff, tax & VAT. Updated annually. 120 pages with many illustrations.

By **Peter Hingston**   ISBN 0 906555 20 5   **£8.50**

The Best Accounts Books
For non-VAT (and VAT) registered Small Businesses

Launched in 1991 and recently updated, these books are now used by tens of thousands of businesses around the UK. Written in layman's language, with a simple and attractive format and full instructions. Suitable for most businesses (sole traders, partnerships or ltd companies). There are two books for non-VAT registered businesses and one for a VAT business. Pages from these books are illustrated in this book (p47 and p50-52). A4 size, hardcovers.

The YELLOW BOOK (for a *cash* business)   ISBN 0 906555 11 6   **£8.99**

The BLUE BOOK (for a *credit* business)   ISBN 0 906555 12 4   **£8.99**

The BLUE VAT BOOK (VAT version)   ISBN 0 906555 14 0   **£11.99**

Please phone if you are in any doubt as to which book you should order.

The Best Small Business Accounts Software
The software mimics the non-VAT accounts books above. Suitable for any PC (not Apple Mac). Specify YELLOW or BLUE version. Supplied on 3½" disk and available by Mail Order only. The price includes (limited) phone support. Easy!   **£39**

HOW TO ORDER

From a Bookshop: Quote them the ISBN number above and ask them to order the book [not software] from us through Teleordering. We usually despatch within 2-3 days. Trade terms.

Mail Order: For books, either phone us with your credit card details, or send a cheque made to "Hingston Publishing Co.", adding **£1.90** for p&p for 1 book (**£2.90** for 2 or 3 books) – UK only. Allow 7-10 days for delivery. For software, please phone. Please note prices may change.

Hingston Publishing Co., Honeymoor Lodge, Eaton Bishop, Hereford HR2 9QT.

Telephone us on: 01981 251621